*The Bishop Henry McNeal Turner Studies
in North American Black Religion
Volume V*

Theodore Walker, Jr.

Empower the People

Social Ethics for the African-American Church

WIPF & STOCK · Eugene, Oregon

Wipf and Stock Publishers
199 W 8th Ave, Suite 3
Eugene, OR 97401

Empower the People
Social Ethics for the African-American Church
By Walker, Theodore, Jr.
Copyright © 1991 Orbis Books All rights reserved.
Softcover ISBN-13: 978-1-6667-5214-4
Hardcover ISBN-13: 978-1-6667-5215-1
Publication date 6/23/2022
Previously published by Orbis Books, 1991

This edition is a scanned facsimile of the original edition published in 1991.

Empower the People

Contents

Abbreviations vii

Acknowledgments ix

Preface xi

Chapter One
Social Location, Social Ethics, and Black Theology   1
   Social Location   1
   Social Ethics and Black Power in Black Theology   10
   Notes   14
   Bibliography   17

Chapter Two
Freedom as Empowerment   20
A Black Theological Conception
   Freedom in Hebrew and Christian Scriptures   20
   Martin Luther King, Jr.'s, Conception of Freedom and the
      Philosophy of Black Power   23
   Freedom according to McKissick's Philosophy of Black
      Nationalism   26
   The Struggle Continues   29
   Notes   30
   Bibliography   32

Chapter Three
The Ethic of Breaking Bread   34
Sociological Descriptions, Predictions, and Socio-Ethical Prescriptions
   for Liberal Coalition Efforts
   Let Us Break Bread Together   34
   The African-American Circumstance in the 1980s and Liberal
      Public Policy Prescriptions for the 1990s   36
   Notes   49
   Bibliography   50

Chapter Four
The Fruitful Multiplication of Righteousness 52
Analyzing Liberal Coalition Agenda from the Churchly Perspective of Black Theology
  Liberal Coalition Efforts according to King, McKissick, and Carmichael-Hamilton   52
  Exclusive Concern for U.S. Citizens as a Problem   56
  Liberal Views on Strengthening Black Families   58
  War on Drugs and Crime   64
  Nonviolence as Part of the Liberal Agenda   67
  Notes   67
  Bibliography   71

Chapter Five
Power to the People 73
Sociological Descriptions, Predictions, and Socio-Ethical Prescriptions for the Exercise of Black Power
  The Witness of the Music   74
  The Witness of the People   78
  Social Ethical Prescriptions   82
  Notes   95
  Bibliography   99

Chapter Six
Servant of the People 102
Analyzing Black Power Agenda from the Churchly Perspective of Black Theology
  Religious Ritual: Let the People Dance   103
  Socialization and Education   106
  Reflection on Family Liberation   110
  Leadership and Economic Empowerment   112
  The Bottom Line   120
  Notes   121
  Bibliography   123

Postscript   *127*

Index   *130*

Abbreviations

AC	*African Civilizations*, Graham Connah
ACA	*Ancient Civilizations of Africa*, Cheikh Anta Diop
AE	"An Agenda for Empowerment," Marian W. Edelman
AMX	*The Autobiography of Malcolm X*
BFSC	"The Black Family: Socialization and Conflict," Delores P. Aldridge
BLC	*Black Leaders in Conflict*, Peter J. Paris
BMFR	"Black Male-Female Relationships," Osei-Mensah Aborampah
BP	*Black Power*, Stokeley Carmichael and Charles V. Hamilton
BPA	*The Black Preacher in America*, Charles V. Hamilton
BPLT	*Beyond Preference: Liberation Theories of Independent Associations*, Franklin I. Gamwell
CBSP	*Crisis in Black Sexual Politics*, Nathan and Julia Hare, eds.
CCR	*Civilities and Civil Rights*, William H. Chafe
CLBF	*The Church in the Life of the Black Family*, Wallace C. Smith
CNI	*The Crisis of the Negro Intellectual*, Harold Cruse
CORE	Congress of Racial Equality
EBF	*The Endangered Black Family*, Nathan and Julia Hare
MVBW	"Moral Values and Black Womanists," Toinette E. Eugene
NCBC	National Committee of Black Churchmen
NCNC	National Committee of Negro Churchmen
PBE	*Plural But Equal*, Harold Cruse
PF	*Prophetic Fragments*, Cornel West
RBF	*Roots of a Black Future*, J. Deotis Roberts
RPG	"Religion, Politics, and Gender," Evelyn Brooks
SBA/89	*The State of Black America 1989*, National Urban League
SCLC	Southern Christian Leadership Conference
SNCC	Student Nonviolent Coordinating Committee
ST	*The Social Teachings of the Black Churches*, Peter J. Paris
TD	*The Truly Disadvantaged*, William J. Wilson

TFM	*Three Fifths of a Man*, Floyd McKissick
TR	*There is a River*, Vincent Harding
UNIA	Universal Negro Improvement Association
WDWGFH	*Where Do We Go From Here*, Martin Luther King, Jr.
WGS	"Welcome to Gladiator School," Lawrence Gonzalez

Acknowledgments

In addition to the authors of the various works that I refer to, there are many other persons in the scholarly academy to whom I am indebted for contributions to the development of this text. I can name only a proximate few. Among them are my teachers, including Charles H. Long (who first inspired and empowered a University of North Carolina undergraduate to pursue a scholarly vocation), Philip E. Devenish, Stanley Hauerwas, and John H. Yoder; my colleagues at the Perkins School of Theology, and previously at Bethune-Cookman College and at Hood Theological Seminary at Livingstone College, especially Dean Frank Brown at Hood. From among my colleagues at the Perkins School of Theology, those who contributed time and attention to answering my queries about some point I cared to address in this text are Joseph L. Allen, William Farmer, Frederick Carney, Victor Furnish, David Maldonado, Schubert Ogden, Thomas Spann, James Thomas, James Ward, and Yap Kim Hao. Including my colleagues on other faculties, Vincent Harding, Stanley Hauerwas, Schubert Ogden, and Yap Kim Ho offered critical comments on major portions of early drafts. Those who offered critical commentary on subsequent drafts are William Farmer, David Maldonado, Klaus Penzel, and Edward Poitras. James H. Cone and William R. Burrows were most helpful in preparing the final version for publication. Joseph L. Allen and Philip E. Devenish were generous enough to read and critique almost every page of almost every draft. Special thanks to them. Mortimer Arias, Riggins Earl, Cain H. Felder, James Kirby, Jacqueline Grant, and Zan W. Holmes are among those who on various occasions provided a few well chosen words, which made important differences in the development and publication of this text. And there is hardly a page, note, or word that did not benefit from the attention of Paul Glasser-Kerr (research assistant). From other parts of the university: Tom Downing, Dave Gagnon, John Wesley Johnson, Terry Smith, and Robert J. Smith helped me in managing the computer technology, and Lillie Jenkins-Carter along with the staff at Bridwell and Fondren libraries provided important assistance. And of course I am indebted to the Perkins School of Theology and Southern Methodist University for providing me with the reduced teaching load, administrative support, research assistance, research leave, and other resources that made it possible to complete this text in a timely fashion.

Also from the world of universities and colleges, there are my students.

Much of what is said in this text is the fruit of what I have learned from dialogue with students at the Perkins School of Theology and in Southern Methodist University's Ph.D. program, and at Bethune-Cookman College and Hood Theological Seminary—including especially those with whom I studied the Bible.

From the world of family and friends, I am indebted to LeVonne Baird-Bridges for original historical research concerning the tribe of Zebulan Vance Woods, to Juanita Charles for pointing me to sources pertaining to the black African identity of ancient Egyptians, to Jerry Walker for reading and critiquing early drafts, to Kenneth Walker and Derek Brinson for teaching me about attention to the witness of our music, to my father, Rev. Theodore Walker, Sr., whose preaching provided me with my earliest and best theological education, to my mother, Mary Edna Woods Walker, and to the whole tribe of Walker, and the whole tribe of Woods. Also I am indebted to Patricia Francies for research and editorial assistance, to Linda Brown and Glora Tate Reed for critical commentary, and to Rev. Eugene Belcher, Dr. Mary Palmore, attorney Marvel Daniels, and Brenda Bulger Walker for inspiration.

From my churchly affiliations, I am indebted to St. Luke "Community" United Methodist Church in Dallas, Texas (Rev. Zan W. Holmes, pastor), for being my churchly home-away-from-home and to Shiloh Baptist Church in Greensboro, North Carolina (Rev. Otis Hairston, pastor) and Allen Chapel African Methodist Episcopal Church in Roxboro, North Carolina (Rev. Marion B. Robinson, pastor), for being my churchly homes at home.

Preface

This is not leisure reading. A measure of disciplined study is required. Two of the six chapters—3 and 5—are extended and sometimes detailed descriptions of scholarly socio-scientific and social ethical literature. Chapter 3 is a description of social ethical views from the literature of black liberal sociology published during the 1980s. Chapter 5 is a description of social ethical views from the literature of black power oriented social science published during the 1980s. The black liberal views described in chapter 3 are evaluated from a black churchly perspective in chapter 4. The black power views described in chapter 5 are evaluated from a black churchly perspective in chapter 6. Also, citations and endnotes are extensive. In many instances, my purpose is to refer to relevant literature and in some instances to provide further discussion of a particular point. The chapter titles, subtitles, subheadings, and italicized text are important navigational instruments.

CHAPTER ONE

Social Location, Social Ethics, and Black Theology

This book is about political theory, sociology, and social ethics. It is written from an African-American churchly perspective. Accordingly, it is classified as a work in black theological social ethics.

SOCIAL LOCATION

It is customary to introduce oneself prior to engaging in conversation. This is partly because who one is makes some difference to what one says and to how what one says is understood. Inasmuch as our sisters and brothers in Latin America and elsewhere have reminded us that this applies to theological discourse as well as to any other, let us begin with an introduction—which is also a statement of collective self-understanding and social location.

We Are African-Americans

I am an African-American. I was born on the continent of North America, in the United States, in the state of North Carolina, in the city of Greensboro, in 1953. Before I could even write my own name, my parents—my father, Rev. Theodore D. Walker, Sr., and my mother, Mary Edna Woods Walker—taught me to scribble the word "Greensboro" by pointing to the masthead of the daily newspaper. The people of my father's house and tribe are the descendants of enslaved people from the continent of Africa. We are separated from the mother continent by an indeterminate number of generations. As for my mother's people, we are separated from our motherland by only a few generations. At our July 1988 family reunion in Roxboro, North Carolina, the eldest members of the Woods tribe were from the generation of my maternal grandfather, Zebulon Vance Woods (1876–1972). They continued to recall that their grandfather—Moses D.

Woods I—was a resident of Africa until he was forcefully removed from that continent and sold as a slave to an Anglo-American plantation owner—one Hugh Woods (1783–1863) from near Roxboro, North Carolina.[1] With respect to the eldest living members of the Woods tribe, there are only two or three generations between Roxboro and Africa. In cross-generational terms, the tribes of Woods and of Walker are African and American. This is typical of our people, and therefore we call ourselves "African-Americans."

In describing ourselves as African-Americans we are thinking across continents and generations. We are referencing both land and blood. We refer to the continental land masses of Africa and of America, and at the same time we refer to the blood or biogenetic and other inheritance we have received from African peoples. We have inherited the blood of Africans.

If we were to conceive of ourselves across a great many more generations, we would discover that all humans have inherited the blood of Africans. According to the prevailing scientific evidence, all humans have inherited African blood in the sense that human evolution and civilization has its genesis on the African continent. In the more specifically biogenetic sense, all of us are genetically descended from a single African woman we now call "Eve."[2] In these more inclusive senses, all Americans are African-Americans. But as most of us use the language, those who are commonly called African-Americans are those Americans who have a biogenetic connection with certain darker peoples of Africa, which is much more direct and recent (reaching across fewer generations) than is the case for a pedigreed Anglo-Saxon. It is in reference to this more recent African blood that we call ourselves African-Americans.

We Are Black

It is characteristic of Americans with recent African blood to have a dark to black (melanin rich) skin color. This black skin is the most visible mark of African blood. Just as we witness to an African inheritance in speaking of ourselves as African-American, so too we witness to this same inheritance and more when we speak of ourselves as black.

When we think of ourselves in terms of color, we invoke the tradition of classifying people according to a color gradation ranging from black to white and associated with skin color. Skin color is determined by the skin's melanin content. People with the highest melanin levels have the darkest skin and are at the black end of the spectrum. At the extreme other end are people with pale melanin-deficient skin, for which they are called "pale face" or white. Between the extremes of melanin richness and melanin deficiency there are the middle ranges, which along with black are collectively termed "colored" for people of color (nonwhites if you please), and which are frequently delineated as yellow, brown, red, and black.

The greatest difficulty with this kind of color consciousness is that, in the North Atlantic cultures at least, it is frequently translated willy-nilly into some utterly untenable theory of race. Among the more widespread of these untenable theories of race are those that translate the white-colored-black spectrum into a Caucasoid-Mongoloid-Negroid typology. Then there are a host of theories that correlate these alleged racial typologies with linguistic typologies and other variables. Most of these various theories of race have a racist and Euro-centric character usually associated with a color-coded view of the world as a world in which "white" is the sign of the good, the true, the beautiful, even the divine. At the other and lower end of reality there is the bad, the ugly, the immoral, the criminal, even the satanic—the black.

This philosophy of white supremacy is deeply embedded in North Atlantic culture. When this absurd and immoral philosophy is superimposed upon a color-coded sociology, ethnology, and historiography, the result is a community of theory so filled with prejudice, ethnocentrism, superiority complexes, malicious intent, ignorance, ingenious gerrymandering, bad faith, intent to deceive, and the like, as to render questionable the value of nearly all North Atlantic academic race theory.

The value of most of what North Atlantic historical studies contribute to the conversation is betrayed by its own arbitrary and outlandish conforming of the data to the demarcations drawn by prejudice in favor of a philosophy of white supremacy. For example, highly regarded historians, Egyptologists, and archeologists have falsely separated white from black, Caucasoid from Negroid, proto-European from Nubian, Eurasian from African, at the Tropic of Cancer. Below the Tropic of Cancer it is said that one finds the culture of black Africans; but everything in ancient Africa that is north of the Tropic of Cancer is said to be white or approximately European in origin and culture. So Akhenaten and Tutankhamen and all our ancestors in North Africa and greater North Africa except for Nubian slaves are described as Caucasian, Caucasoid, white Egyptian, dark Mediterranean, brown Mediterranean, red, brown, yellow, polyglot, Euro-Mediterranean, Euro-African, Eurasian, Indo-European, or what have you; but not as black and African. Of course we recognize this as a bad faith gerrymander designed to describe the world in a way that is consistent with a philosophy of white supremacy and the Euro-centric historiography that accompanies it.[3]

Even many of the most highly regarded contemporary North Atlantic scholars have not yet been liberated from this thoroughly outdated and incontestably wrong hypothesis. For example, there is the Cambridge University Press 1987 publication of Graham Connah's *African Civilizations: Precolonial Cities and States in Tropical Africa: An Archaeological Perspective*. Connah's work is praiseworthy insofar as it succeeds in its effort to contribute to the liberation of "the reading public of the English-speaking world" from the commonly held but false view that "precolonial tropical

African societies" never achieved the "high order" of "cultural complexity" required to produce cities and states. Connah holds "that tropical Africa also attained cultural complexity of a high order" (AC p. ix), and part of the evidence for this view comes from the archeological study of the material remains of precolonial cities and states in tropical Africa. So far, very good. But those of us who are black and African, who have kin and ancestors who lived and continue to live beyond the tropical regions of Africa, must immediately ask why Connah has circumscribed his work in the field of "African archaeology" by reference to the tropics, rather than by reference to the continent of Africa.

Connah answers precisely this question in a section called "Coverage of this book" (AC pp. 20–22). Here he recognizes that there is "an obvious problem with this choice of subject matter in that it excludes North Africa and most of Egypt" (AC p. 21). Connah goes on to explain his preference for an obviously problematic demarcation by saying, "In the case of this book, the intention has been to look at the cities and states of *black* Africa" (AC p. 21). Connah reasons that because he is concerned to discuss the cities and states of black Africa, "therefore, the area considered in this book is defined as 'tropical Africa'. . . . Africa between the Tropic of Cancer and the Tropic of Capricorn" (AC p. 21). Without recourse to even a single piece of supporting evidence of any kind, let alone archeological evidence, Connah supposes that ancient and antiquitous, African peoples to the north of 23.5 degrees north latitude could not have been black. Black Africans, it is supposed, lived only in the tropics.

If Connah and the many North Atlantic scholars who continue to subscribe to this view would consult the material remains of ancient North Africans along the Nile and elsewhere, as well as relevant primary and secondary historical sources, they would find their supposition—that the tropical latitudes distinguish between blacks and whites, or between blacks and nonblacks, along the Nile and elsewhere in early African history—to be wholly and utterly unsubstantiated. To be sure, they would discover that the stones, the bones, the blood, the script, as well as linguistic, historical, and other evidence, testify against their supposition. Our best physical and historical evidence teaches us that in ancient and prehistoric times the predominant peoples of North Africa and greater North Africa were black.[4] In the utter absence of credible evidence to the contrary, there is no good reason not to suppose that any history of people in this area and during these generations is the history of black and colored peoples.

Black Inclusively Conceived

As opposed to the many North Atlantic variations on the theme of white supremacy, it is the habit of the people who describe themselves as black and as African-American to conceive of their blackness so as to reach across generations and continents (blood and land), beyond the "X" in Malcolm

X, so as to include the biogenetic and other inheritance from Africans whose blood is marked by melanin-rich skin and other African features. Moreover, this inclusive reach is not circumscribed by the tropical regions of Africa, or by Semitic language structures, or by the presence of written language, or by monotheistic religion, or by metal technology, or any of the other variables that have been used to define all black Africans to the north of the Tropic of Cancer as other than black and African. If we follow the melanin-rich skin and blood of African peoples through past generations and across sea and land, we must include in the category of blackness not only our common primordial and prehistorical ancestors, but also the historical figures of Akhenaten (Iknaton) and Tutankhamen (King Tut) — indeed, the entirety of ancient Egypt's Old Kingdom, and virtually all of the Middle and New Kingdoms until the Ptolemies. We must also include among the black peoples of ancient North and greater North Africa many biblical and Semitic and other African and Afro-Asiatic tribes. And furthermore, we should not fail to recognize the existence of ancient black peoples in southeast Asia.[5] Indeed, the traditional Hindu depictions of the Lord Krishna (whose name means "the black one") with a melanin-rich blue-black skin color, as well as the dark skin and hair of many contemporary southern Indians, continue to affirm the historical and archeological evidence for the ancient presence of black people in southern Asia.

Rather than continuing with the clearly racist academic habit of trying to conceive of the ancient peoples of North Africa, the Arabian Peninsula, and southern India under the rubric of white-European culture by describing them as "oriental-European" or "Indo-European," we prefer to speak of the ancient peoples of North Africa as African, and to acknowledge the presence of black and colored peoples with obviously African ancestry along the Mediterranean, throughout the Arabian Peninsula, and in southern Asia by speaking also of the Afro-Mediterranean world, of greater North Africa, and of the Afro-Asiatic world.[6]

This inclusive understanding of blackness sounds a note of protest and revolution vis-à-vis the philosophy of white superiority and black inferiority. This protest and revolution was made explicit during the development of the philosophy of black power in the 1960s. Perhaps the most significant and enduring achievement of the black power movement is that it enabled African-Americans in general to change their minds about the disdain and degradation of black and blackness inherited from Anglo-American culture.

Prior to the black power movement, in many circles the polite and inoffensive way to refer to Americans with recent African blood was to speak of them as "colored" or "Negro," but not as "black." Black was an insult. Black people preferred not to be called black, and white people preferred that the term "black" function only to degrade and insult. But when we internalized the philosophy of black power, we protested and revolted against the understanding that black was shameful and ugly. Instead, we affirmed that "black is beautiful" and that one can be "black and proud."

A people who had for a time been ashamed of African blood and of blackness became proud of African rootage and blackness. Thereafter we declined to describe ourselves as colored and Negro in favor of describing ourselves as black and African-American. When we affirm blackness, inclusively conceived—that is, across generations and continents—we make use of color consciousness in a way that stands in protest to the prevailing color-coded philosophy of white supremacy and its associated theories of race and history. We may speak of this change in our color consciousness as a revolution of the mind.

We Are Not a Minority

Because we conceive of ourselves as black and as African-American rather than as simply U.S. citizens with a darker complexion, we do not always conceive of ourselves as a minority. The minority status of black and colored peoples is a strictly local phenomenon.

When we conceive of ourselves in ways that do not exclude black and colored peoples outside the U.S.A., we cannot fail to see that we are not a minority people. But even within the United States, demographic distribution has not been static. There are many places where we are now the majority. Washington, D.C., for example, is seventy percent black. And according to present demographic projections, the time when peoples of color will be the majority population for much more, and in time all, of the U.S.A. is not more than a few generations away. With regard to the U.S. population, demographic revolution is upon us now.

Present and recent generations in the North Atlantic nations are not in the habit of perceiving a present, a future, or a past, in which white people are not the majority and dominant culture. When North Atlantic whites project or imagine the world of their descendants in the future, the projections and images are almost always contrary to demographic reality. For example, the science fiction and other visionary hypotheses produced by whites in the U.S.A. and elsewhere in the North Atlantic world, with hardly a single exception, depict a predominantly white future. Gene Roddenberry's *Star Trek* and the current *Star Trek: The Next Generation*, along with *Alien* and *2001* and *2010* and *Star Wars* and *Dune* and nearly any other envisionment of the future produced by whites in the U.S.A. will show us a world that consists predominantly of white people.

As for the past, again, North Atlantic culture usually thinks in terms of a predominantly white world. For example, in the United States, what is usually called "world history" could as well be called "the history of white people," because it is an account of history that excludes concern for colored and black peoples except insofar as they come into contact with white people. Moreover, it is typically conceived that biblical narratives are predominantly about white people. Jesus, Solomon, David, Moses, Pharaoh, Abraham, Noah, Adam, and Eve are virtually always conceived and depicted as white. Even when it is granted that a Jew or Hebrew might be found among biblical peoples, it is still, almost unanimously, supposed that biblical Hebrews and Jews could never have been Afro-Asiatic and black. North Atlantic culture, including its learned academies and religious communities, is in the habit of treating the past and history as mainly the history of white people, most particularly the history of white men.

A less racist vision of the past, of our present world, and of the emerging world compels us to recognize that we African-Americans are part of the largely colored and black Third World majority. When we conceive of ourselves in ways that reach beyond the present generation and beyond present state and national borders, we cannot fail to perceive that we are not simply a minority. Given a more inclusive, cross-generational and global perspective, we are part of the Third World majority.

Our Liberation Colors: Red, Black, Green, and Gold

When we African-Americans think of ourselves, we think in the language of struggle for freedom and liberation. Such thinking is nicely symbolized by our liberation colors. Our liberation flag, which was popularized by Marcus Garvey (1887-1940) and the Universal Negro Improvement Association, and which came to be strongly identified with the black power movement of the 1960s and 70s in the United States, is red, black, and green. Red is for the blood, especially the blood sacrificed to the struggle for freedom. Black is for the people. Green is for the land, particularly the motherland of Africa. These liberation colors, and our liberation flag, are widely recognized symbols for our struggle.[7]

During the 1980s we became increasingly inclined to add a fourth liberation color—gold. Gold is for the wealth that was stolen from the motherland of Africa. This wealth includes not only mineral and other natural resources like diamonds and gold, but also the more than fifty million people and their descendants stolen from Africa during the transatlantic slave trade. We black people in America are part of that stolen wealth. Similarly, the attempt to exclude ancient black peoples north of the Tropic of Cancer from the continent of Africa and from the category of blackness is another instance of white supremacy stealing wealth from black Africa. The reclaiming of this and other stolen legacy[8] is an important part of the liberation agenda symbolized by the color gold.

The color gold is recognized by our sisters and brothers in Azania-South Africa and in the front-line states of Angola, Tanzania, Zambia, Mozambique, and Zimbabwe. The flag of the African National Congress, for example, is black, green, and gold. Numerous other African countries have national flags using gold along with two and sometimes three of the other colors—red, black, and green. Our sisters and brothers from islands that white folk once thought to be just west of India (the so-called "West Indies") recognize all four liberation colors. Jamaican Rastafarians, for example, recognize the national colors of Jamaica as black, gold, and green. Because of their religious and political consciousness of Ethiopia, they recognize Ethiopia's national colors of green, gold, and red. The pan-African unity of mind between the black consciousness movement in southern Africa, the Garvey consciousness of African-Americans in the Caribbean, the black power movement in North America, and the pan-African liberation agenda of black peoples everywhere, is affirmed in the fact that Africans in the Americas and elsewhere are now starting to display liberation flags with all four colors. In North America, usually these flags have three horizontal stripes—from top to bottom—of red, black, and green, and a vertical stripe or border of gold. African-Americans and Africans all over the planet now recognize four liberation colors.

These liberation colors—red, black, green, and gold—symbolize a self-understanding inclusive enough to reach across national and continental boundaries so as to accept Africa as our motherland and her people as our people. It is inclusive enough to reach across generations so as to acknowledge our inheritance from Africans back beyond the generation Malcolm called "X," and it does not exclude black peoples of antiquity and the ancient world who lived north of tropical or sub-Sahara Africa. This cross-generational self-understanding includes generations of the past, from whom we have inherited much, and generations of the future, to whom we must contribute what will ensure their social and spiritual well-being.

We Are a Church People

There is more. Genealogy, ethnology, historiography, geography, and liberation philosophy do not adequately describe us. It is essential to see that we are religious people. God-consciousness is an essential part of our self-understanding.[9] It is the tradition of Africans almost everywhere to conceive of ourselves always in relation to God.

Traditionally, the majority of religious African-Americans in the United States have been associated with churches in the Protestant denominations. For example, I and the people of my father's house are members of Shiloh Baptist Church in Greensboro, North Carolina (Rev. Otis Hairston, pastor), a church affiliated with the National Baptist Convention, U.S.A. My mother's people belong to Allen Chapel in Roxboro, North Carolina (Rev. Marion B. Robinson, pastor), an African Methodist Episcopal Church. How then does our religious and denominational heritage fit with our red-black-green-gold liberation agenda?

The Black Church Revolution

The most basic North American church history teaches us that African-American Protestant churches are not "Protestant" in the sense of having been born in protest to alleged Catholic abuses. Instead, African-American churches are "protestant" in the very different sense of having been born in protest against domination and oppression by white Euro-American Protestant denominations and churches.

Typically, African-Americans retained the name of whichever denomination or church we happened to have stood in protest against. For example, the African Methodist Episcopal Church is called "Methodist" largely on account of the fact that white officers and members of St. George Methodist Episcopal Church in Philadelphia were so oppressive of their black members that in 1787 the black members, under the leadership of a former slave—Richard Allen (for whom Allen Chapel is named)—separated themselves from that white congregation and formed their own independent black church. At first the new protesting church called itself "the Free African Society." Then in 1816, it became "the African Methodist Episcopal Church." The churches which are descended from African-American congregations that stood in protest to control by white Methodists are now found mainly among these African-American Methodist groups: the African Methodist Episcopal Church, the African Methodist Episcopal Zion Church, and the Christian Methodist Episcopal Church. The churches which are descended from African-American congregations that stood in protest to control by white Baptists are now found mainly among these African-American Baptist groups: the National Baptist Convention, U.S.A., Inc., the National Baptist Convention of America, and the Progressive National Baptist Convention. Most other African-American denominations and racially separated churches have a similar heritage.

When the many petitions by African-Americans for integration into Anglo-American churches on an egalitarian basis failed, African-Americans responded by withdrawing en masse and forming their own independent black churches. Black congregations were thereby empowered to enjoy a freedom of worship and self-determination that was denied them within white ecclesial structures. This radical movement of protest, schism, separation, and reformation is described here as the black church revolution.

When we African-Americans conceive of ourselves across generations sufficient to include this churchly heritage, we cannot fail to think in terms of radical and revolutionary struggle. To be sure, Gayraud S. Wilmore's classic work *Black Religion and Black Radicalism: An Interpretation of the Religious History of Afro-American People* teaches us that, throughout our history, African-American churches and religions have been a relentless source of "radical thrusts" for liberation. Moreover, we cannot fail to remember that the civil rights movement and the black power movement were virtually born in our churches.[10] The history of African-American churches must be told in the language of radical and revolutionary struggle for religious and secular liberty. Radical and revolutionary struggle for liberation, for justice, and for empowerment is at the very heart of our religious heritage. The radical heritage of the black church revolution is consistent with the liberation agenda symbolized by our red-black-green-gold liberation colors.

We are then an ethnos or people who conceive of ourselves across space and time so as to affirm that we are both African and American. We are black. We are the descendants of enslaved Africans and of other historical and prehistorical black African peoples north and south of the Tropic of Cancer. We are among the majority of the world's people of color, many of whom are struggling against the continuing heritage of North Atlantic captivity and socio-economic-political and military oppression. And very importantly, most of us conceive of ourselves as a people in relation to God. Consequently, any political theory or social ethic that can hope to be acceptable in our communities must be consistent with our religious heritage. It is, therefore, to the good that this work is being done by a theologian. *The purpose of this book is to present a conception of freedom/liberty and a liberating social ethic relentlessly informed by a black churchly understanding of ourselves in relation to God.*

SOCIAL ETHICS AND BLACK POWER IN BLACK THEOLOGY

In the strictest sense, all ethics is social ethics as all human behavior is social behavior. But to speak of ethics as social ethics is to announce an emphasis upon collective, institutional, structural, and other macroscopic relations and societal habits to the relative neglect of microscopic or individual and small group relations.

Social ethical reflection has descriptive, predictive, prescriptive, and interpretive aspects. The descriptive aspect of social ethical reflection consists usually in socio-scientific or sociological descriptions of conditions and circumstances pertaining to a given population. Such socio-scientific descriptions are understood to have a predictive character, which is sometimes explicit, at other times implicit. In a manner not unlike that of natural science generally, socio-scientific descriptions of present circumstances are understood to contribute to our ability to forecast future conditions. Frequently social science comes to us in a formula such as this: If said condition or trend continues, then we can expect the following. "What is" is understood to be partly determinative of "what will be." The prescriptive aspect enters on account of our value judgments about "what should be," and accordingly, what we "ought" or "should" do.

Our value judgments contribute to the shaping of our descriptions, predictions, and prescriptions. Value judgments are part of the interpretive aspect of social ethical reflection. Given particular value judgments and other interpretive instruments and influences (for example, God-consciousness), we may conclude that we ought to do this or that to bring or keep present and future circumstances in line with what, according to our interpretation and value judgments, should be. Often, in the social sciences the descriptive and predictive tasks are pursued to the relative neglect of interpretive judgments and explicit social ethical prescriptions. Nevertheless, explicit or not, socio-scientific analysis employs interpretive instruments inclusive of value judgments. Many—perhaps most, if not all—sociological descriptions and predictions entail at least implicit prescriptions (an implicit "ought"). It is the responsibility of the social ethical disciplines to systematically explicate these otherwise implicit interpretive and prescriptive aspects.

Our social location in the 1990s, and through the generations of the great African diaspora, is appropriately described in the language of enslavement and oppression. Given this social location, when we think in terms of social ethical prescriptions, the desired end is to contribute to the increase of freedom/liberty and opportunity for all (including future generations). To be sure, Vincent Harding finds that "the active black struggle for freedom and justice" is "the central theme" of black history in the United States (*There is a River: The Black Struggle for Freedom in America*, p. xx). Accordingly, the social ethic most appropriate to our experience and aspirations would be a social ethic of freedom. Freedom or liberty is the central interpretive theme for our social ethical reflections.

Political scientists and many African-Americans can recall that in 1967 Stokely Carmichael (now known as Kwame Ture) and Prof. Charles V. Hamilton (then chairman of the department of political science at Roosevelt University in Chicago, and currently professor of government at Columbia University) published *Black Power: The Politics of Liberation in America*. This text in political science is not simply a description of the political aspects of African-American social existence in the U.S.A.; it is also, intentionally and explicitly, prescriptive as well. The philosophy of black power prescribes an African-American political activity that is separate from traditional political parties, that is controlled by African-Americans, and pursues the liberation of African-Americans and all others through black power—that is, through the political power of independently controlled African-American institutions. *Black Power: The Politics of Liberation in America* engages in social ethical reflection focusing mainly upon the political aspects of our quest for freedom.

Carmichael and Hamilton follow in the tradition of academic political science and of social scientific disciplines generally in that their work exhibits no consciousness of our relation to God, and in that they offer hardly more than an occasional reference to the religious and churchly aspects of African-American existence. But our social location is such that in order for us to find the social ethical prescriptions of political science acceptable, they must be consistent with our religious experience.

The Exodus-Joshua-Jesus traditions and the tradition of the black church revolution are examples "from the black experience" of liberating social activities, which include separation from enslaving and oppressive social structures, and reformation as an independently empowered people. In North America the idea of a black withdrawal from oppressive white social structures, of separation rather than integration, in favor of the formation of autonomous black institutions and structures originated with black religious communities. And later, black power advocates who had the experience of working in a civil rights movement that was lead and peopled by African-American churches (for instance, on a number of occasions, Stokely Carmichael worked with Martin Luther King, Jr.) sought to extend the liberating social behavior of black religion into the political arena. The black church revolution was one of the earliest successful expressions of black empowerment by enslaved Africans and their descendants in the North American diaspora. (And it may be that this was the first largely nonviolent revolution in North American history since the discovery of Columbus by native peoples who were not really Indians.)

It is therefore no surprise that black power philosophy would have emerged from a liberation struggle (the civil rights movement) centered in black religious congregations. Just as black religious communities achieved liberation from oppression through a policy of separation and reformation rather than through integration and accommodation, the modern advocates of black power seek political freedom by withdrawing from the prevailing white dominated political structures and parties, and forming independently empowered and black controlled political structures and parties. Racial separation, consolidation, reformation, and exercise of independent black power has long been part of our churchly understanding of progress toward freedom; and here lately it has become part of our political quest for freedom. Black power, then, is the child of black religion. Yet insofar as black power advocates follow in the tradition of North Atlantic academic political and social science by being neglectful of religious and churchly matters, we may describe black power as a wayward child of black religion.

Black church leaders had extended welcoming and affirming arms to its wayward child as early as 1966—the very same year that Carmichael and Willie Ricks first introduced "Black Power!" as a slogan in the civil rights movement. I refer in particular to the "Black Power Statement" by the National Committee of Negro Churchmen published in the July 31, 1966 issue of the *New York Times*. In this statement African-American church leaders affirmed that the problem of racial oppression was about an "imbalance of power and conscience"—the "conscienceless power" of white America confronting the "powerless conscience" of black America. The statement also points to the black church as prototype and "to some extent" the actual presence of black power; and it prescribes extending the presence of black power into political and economic areas.[11] In 1967 the National Committee of Negro Churchmen (NCNC) changed its name to the National Committee of Black Churchmen (NCBC). The change from "Negro" to "Black" indicated a further affirmation of the militant valuation of blackness, which characterized the black power movement.

African-American ministers and church leaders from the full spectrum of black congregational life were quick to welcome the philosophy of black power. The resulting appropriation of black power by black theologians produced a body of theological literature called "black theology." Among the classic theological appropriations of black power are James H. Cone's *Black Theology and Black Power* and *Black Theology of Liberation*. The religious appropriation of the philosophy of black power has become an essential and defining feature of modern black theology.[12] *Insofar as black theology is true to its appropriation of the philosophy of black power, and true to the heritage of the black church revolution, the social ethics of freedom and black empowerment is its proper and essential business.*

This work is unlike most of the literature in the field of social ethics. It is distinguished from most of the field in that its social descriptions of Afro-America are mainly self-descriptions, and also in that its social prescriptions are addressed to African-Americans. We are not here addressing ourselves to government, to philanthropists, to public policy-makers, or to other predominantly non-African-American institutions and groups. We address hardly more than a word or two to white people. This is a self-instructional gesture. Rather than being unduly concerned with what others say about African-Americans, or with what others should do about the circumstance of African-Americans, we are more concerned with how we African-Americans understand ourselves and others, and with what we African-Americans ought to do for ourselves and others. Social ethics of this sort comes under the category of black power. The philosophy of black power, as described by Carmichael and Hamilton, is about black folk taking care of black folk's business (BP p. vii). We are about black folk and in particular black churches taking care of black folk's business. Black theological social ethics aspires to contribute to the increase of liberty or freedom for all through the righteous exercise of black power, most especially the power of black churches.[13]

Another distinctive feature of black theological social ethical reflection is that we do not fail to employ our preaching voice. In most scholarly social ethical reflection, the voice of the preacher is rarely heard; but in this work, not only do we refer to the words and deeds of our preachers, we also make use of the preaching genre in presenting some aspects of our social ethical reflection. This is consistent with the fact that black theological social ethical reflection is nourished by black churchly traditions, and it is consistent with our effort to speak in a voice that is most welcome among our church people.

The language of "black theological social ethics" serves to locate our reflections within the scholarly academy, but this language does not adequately express the spirit and soul of our enterprise. For such better expression, let us recover the language of ancient north and greater North African religions—the language of prophecy. The biblical prophet, we recall, interprets the world in terms of relationship to God, and preaches a relentlessly God-conscious social ethic. The prophet describes the circumstance of the people in terms of the consequences of unrighteous behavior. The prophet predicts that if we continue in the ways of unrighteousness, our future and that of our descendants will be one of increased misfortune, suffering, and death—that is, "the wages of sin." And so the prophet prescribes that we should repent and take up the practice and habits of righteousness, of obedience to God's will, so as to contribute to the possibility of a more favorable future. In this sense, black theological social ethical reflection takes the form of religious prophecy.[14]

NOTES

1. See Madeline Hall Eaker, ed., *The Heritage of Person County, 1981* (Roxboro, N.C.: Person County Historical Society, n.d.; Winston-Salem, N.C.: Hunter Publishing Company). In the section concerning Moses D. Woods II, prepared by Levone Baird-Bridges, we are told that "his father, Moses D. Woods I, was brought to this country on a ship from Africa and was sold into slavery to Hugh Woods I" (p. 458). In the section on the white Woods family by Nell Woods Mullins, we read that "the Woods were plantation owners, with many slaves" (p. 456). Like many African-Americans, Moses D. Woods I drew his surname from the family for whom he worked as a slave.

2. Here I refer to recent scientific studies of human genetic inheritance indicating that all contemporary humans have a common African female ancestor. Appropriately, this common ancestor is called "Eve." See Douglass Wallace, "The Search for Adam and Eve," *Newsweek*, January 11, 1988. For an account of recent archeological evidence for the African genesis of humankind, one may consult the work of Louis S. B. Leakey, Mary D. Leakey, and more recently the work of Richard Leakey and Kamoya Kimeu. See Richard Leakey and Alan Walker's description of Kimeu's archeological excavations in Kenya in *National Geographic*, vol. 168, no. 5 (November 1985). The combination of genetic and archeological evidence affirms the traditional African assertion that Africa is the "Alkebu-lan" or "Mother of Humanity."

3. W. E. B. DuBois, in his book *The World and Africa: An Inquiry into the Part Which Africa Has Played in World History* (New York: Viking Press, 1947), notes that during the nineteenth century Europeans sought to justify their "right to live upon the labor and poverty of the colored peoples of the world" by using science and history to prove that the white race was superior to others, and that "everything really successful in human culture was white.... In order to prove this, even black people in India and Africa were labeled as 'white' if they showed any trace of progress" (p. 20). This unfortunate tradition continues in the North Atlantic academy to the present day.

4. For hard scientific data showing conclusively that the ancient Egyptians were black, see Cheikh Anta Diop, "Origin of the Ancient Egyptians," *Ancient Civilizations of Africa*, G. Mokhtar, ed., which is volume 2 of the UNESCO 8-volume *General History of Africa* (Paris: United Nations Educational, Scientific, and Cultural Organization/University of California Press, 1981). Diop examines empirical data and evidence in the following areas: physical anthropology, human images of the protohistorical period, melanin dosage test, osteological measurements, blood groups, writings of classical authors of antiquity, the ancient Egyptians' self-understanding, the witness of the Bible, cultural data, and linguistic affinity. Diop shows

that all these criteria indicate that "the basis of the Egyptian population was negro in the Pre-Dynastic epoch" and that this was the case "from the beginning to the end of Egyptian history" (ACA vol. 2, p. 29). Also, for those who care to see photographic reproductions of the physical remains of ancient Egyptians, see James D. Harris and Edward F. Wente, eds., *X-Ray Atlas of the Royal Mummies* (Chicago: University of Chicago Press, 1980). Analysis of physical remains and other empirical data offer a definitive and univocal affirmation of the black African origin of ancient Egyptian peoples. Similarly, the black African origin of ancient Ethiopian civilization is affirmed by Ephraim Isaac and Cain Hope Felder in their work on ancient Ethiopia, Arabia, and the black Queen of Sheba in "The Origins of Ethiopian Civilization" in *The Proceedings of the International Conference for Ethiopian Studies* (Addis Ababa, 1985). Additionally, Felder offers further reflection on this work in the second chapter—"Ancient Ethiopia and the Queen of Sheba"—of his book *Troubling Biblical Waters: Race, Class, and Family* (Maryknoll, N.Y.: Orbis Books, 1989). In his third chapter—"Racial Motifs in the Biblical Narratives"—Felder's concentration on racial motifs affirms the presence of black African peoples in biblical narratives. The black African presence in biblical narratives is also developed in the work of Charles B. Copher and Randall Bailey. See Charles B. Copher, "The Bible and the African Experience," an unpublished paper presented to the Pan-African Christian Church Conference (July 19, 1988); "Blacks and Jews in Historical Interaction: The Biblical/African Experience," *The Journal of the Interdenominational Theological Center*, vol. 3, no. 1 (Fall 1975); "The Black Man in the Biblical World," *The Journal of the Interdenominational Theological Center*, vol. 1, no. 2 (Spring 1974); "Egypt and Ethiopia in the Old Testament," *Nile Valley Civilizations*, Ivan Van Sertima, ed. (Journal of African Civilizations, Ltd., 1985); "3,000 Years of Biblical Interpretation with Reference to Black Peoples," *The Journal of the Interdenominational Theological Center*, vol. 13, no. 2 (Spring 1986). See also Randall C. Bailey, "Is That Any Name for a Nice Hebrew Boy?: Exodus 2:1-10: the De-Africanization of an Israelite Hero," *The Journal of the Interdenominational Theological Center*, vol. 16 (1989); and see Gene Rice, "The African Roots of the Prophet Zephaniah," *The Journal of Religious Thought*, vol. 36 (Spring-Summer 1979).

5. For scholarly reflection upon the presence of black African people in early Asia, see Ivan Van Sertima and Runoko Rashidi, eds., "African Presence in Early Asia," *The Journal of African Civilizations*, vol. 7, no. 1 (1988); and Ivan Van Sertima and Runoko Rashidi, eds., *African Presence in Early Asia* (New Brunswick, N.J., and Oxford: Transaction Books, 1988).

6. Those who care to consult historical accounts of the presence of black African peoples in regions far removed from tropical Africa should refer to the following: Ivan Van Sertima, ed., *African Presence in Early America* (New Brunswick, N.J.: Transaction Books, 1987); Ivan Van Sertima and Runoko Rashidi, eds., "African Presence in Early Asia," *The Journal of African Civilizations*, vol. 7, no. 1 (1988); Ivan Van Sertima and Runoko Rashidi, eds., *African Presence in Early Asia* (New Brunswick, N.J. and Oxford: Transaction Books, 1988); Ivan Van Sertima, ed., "African Presence in Early Europe," *The Journal of African Civilizations*, vol. 3, no. 1 (1981); idem, ed., *African Presence in Early Europe* (New Brunswick, N.J., and Oxford: Transaction Books, 1985, 1988); idem, *They Came Before Columbus* (New York: Random House, 1976); and also chapter one—"The Ancient World"—of Keith Irvine's *The Rise of the Colored Races* (New York: W. W. Norton, 1970).

7. In March 1921 the Universal Negro Improvement Association (UNIA) issued a "Universal Negro Catechism" prepared by the Reverend George Alexander McGuire (founder of the African Orthodox Church). According to this catechism, red, black, and green were selected as the "National Colors of the Negro Race" at the UNIA First International Negro Convention in New York in August 1920. The catechism, which appears in Robert Hill ed., *Marcus Garvey Universal Negro Improvement Association Papers*, volume 3 (Los Angeles: University of California Press, 1984) reads: "Red is the color of the blood which men must shed for their redemption and liberty; black is the color of the noble and distinguished race to which we belong; green is the color of the luxuriant vegetation of our Motherland" (p. 319).

8. "Stolen legacy" refers to George G. M. James, *Stolen Legacy* (San Francisco: Julian Richardson Associates, 1954, 1988). James argues that "The Greeks were not the authors of Greek philosophy, but the people of North Africa, commonly called the Egyptians." For James, the Western academy's false worship of Greek philosophy, including as it does the denial of ancient black African contributions, is an attempt to steal the legacy of black African peoples. Here James is concerned with reclaiming the heritage that has been stolen by the scholarly expressions of the philosophy of white supremacy, which seek to whiteface the black African civilizations of North Africa, and to deny the black African contributions to the development of Greek and Roman culture. This same theme is the subject of Martin Bernal, *Black Athena: The Afroasiatic Roots of Classical Civilization*, volume 1: *The Fabrication of Ancient Greece 1785–1985* (New Brunswick, N.J.: Rutgers University Press, 1987). On the back cover of the paperback edition, Perry Anderson says of this book: "What is classical about Classical civilization? In one of the most audacious works of scholarship ever written, Martin Bernal challenges the whole basis of our thinking about this question. Classical civilization, he argues, has deep roots in Afroasiatic cultures. But these Afroasiatic influences have been systematically ignored, denied or suppressed since the eighteenth century—chiefly for racist reasons." Bernal is one of only a very few white scholars who publicly acknowledge the continuing racist heritage of the prevailing North Atlantic historiography, and he continues to be almost singularly unique among white scholars on account of his effort to offer a more truthful alternative in this area. Any listing of scholarly literature in this area must include the work of Cheikh Anta Diop and Yosef A. A. ben-Jochannan. From among their many publications, the following are most helpful: Yosef A. A. ben-Jochannan, *Africa: Mother of Western Civilization* (New York: Alkebu-lan Books, 1981/Baltimore: Black Classic Press, 1988); idem, *African Origins of the Major Western Religions* (New York: Alkebu-lan Books, 1970); idem, *Black Man of the Nile and His Family* (New York: Alkebu-lan Books, 1970/Baltimore: Black Classic Press, 1989); Cheikh Anta Diop, *The African Origins of Civilization: Myth or Reality* (New York: Lawrence Hill, 1974).

9. See Walter L. Yates, "The God-consciousness of the Black Church in Historical Perspective" in *Quest for a Black Theology*, James J. Gardiner and J. Deotis Roberts, eds. (Philadelphia: Pilgrim Press, 1971).

10. Gayraud S. Wilmore, *Black Religion and Black Radicalism: An Interpretation of the Religious History of Afro-American People* (Maryknoll, N.Y.: Orbis Books, 1984), is an examination of the historical relationship between black religion and black radicalism in North America. He finds that black religion has a history of nourishing black radicalism. The civil rights movement, black pride, black aware-

ness, black nationalism, pan-Africanism, and black power all have a past in the black churches. This "radical thrust" for liberation is said to be "the defining characteristic of black Christianity and black religion in the United States" (p. x). Wilmore concludes that there is an "inseparable connection" between black religion and black radicalism.

11. See Gayraud S. Wilmore and James H. Cone, *Black Theology: A Documentary History, 1966-1979* (Maryknoll, N.Y.: Orbis Books, 1979). This text contains the National Committee of Negro Churchmen's 1966 black power statement, and other documents and essays pertaining to black churchly appropriations of the philosophy of black power.

12. For most of the North Atlantic theological academy, the term "black theology" would refer to systematic theological appropriations of black power by blacks mainly in the U.S.A. and Canada. As opposed to this prevailing academic habit, I prefer a more global perspective, and a more inclusive understanding of blackness and of black theology. I recognize that "black theology" is inclusive of theological appropriations of black power by African-Americans in Central and South America and by black people on the mother continent, most notably in Azania-South Africa and the frontline states, and elsewhere. Furthermore, black theology in southern Africa is enriched by a native "black consciousness movement"—identified with Steve Beko—which is similar to the "black consciousness" and "black awareness" of African-American black power philosophy. For example, see Allen Aubrey Boesak, *Black Theology Black Power* (Oxford: A.R. Mowbray, 1978). Here Boesak's churchly appropriation of black power is dedicated to his father, mother, wife, and to Steve Beko (p. v). For an extended comparison and contrast of indigenous African and African-American theologies leading to a call for a "pan-African theology," which includes a black feminist perspective, see Josiah U. Young, *Black and African Theologies: Siblings or Distant Cousins?* (Maryknoll, N.Y.: Orbis Books, 1986). Also see Gwinyai Muzorewa, *The Origins and Development of African Theology* (Maryknoll, N.Y.: Orbis Books, 1985); Dwight N. Hopkins, *Black Theology U.S.A. and South Africa: Politics, Culture, and Liberation* (Maryknoll, N.Y.: Orbis Books, 1989).

13. In *Christian Ethics for Black Theology* (Nashville: Abingdon, 1974) Major J. Jones makes "a case for a division of the ethical question" (p. 15). Jones argues that the descendants of slaves and the descendants of slave owners are both bound by the Christian mandate of love, and that this requires each of them to contribute to abolishing the oppressed-oppressor relationship. But the differences between the two social locations imply correspondingly different responses (pp. 16-20). Accordingly, Jones finds that "the ethical question should be divided" (p. 23), and he understands the "attempt to speak ethically from the black side of the question" (p. 18) to be an attempt at "Christian ethics for black theology."

14. Sociologist Robert W. Friedrichs says in chapter three—"Sociology: The Prophetic Mode"—of *A Sociology of Sociology* (New York/Toronto: Free Press/Collier-Macmillan, 1970, 1972) that "sociology, in fact, was born from the loins of prophecy" (p. 69).

BIBLIOGRAPHY

Bailey, Randall C. "Is That Any Name for a Nice Hebrew Boy? Exodus 2:1-10: The De-Africanization of an Israelite Hero." *The Journal of the Interdenominational Theological Center*, vol. 16 (1989).

Bernal, Martin. *Black Athena: The Afroasiatic Roots of Classical Civilization*. Vol. 1, *The Fabrication of Ancient Greece 1785–1985*. New Brunswick: Rutgers University Press, 1987.
Boesak, Allen Aubrey. *Black Theology Black Power*. Oxford: A. R. Mowbray, 1978.
Carmichael, Stokely, and Charles V. Hamilton. *Black Power: The Politics of Liberation in America*. New York: Vintage Books, 1967.
Cone, James H. *Black Theology and Black Power*. New York: Seabury Press, 1969.
———. *Black Theology of Liberation*. Philadelphia: Lippincott, 1970.
Connah, Graham. *African Civilizations: Precolonial Cities and States in Tropical Africa: An Archaeological Perspective*. New York and Cambridge: Cambridge University Press, 1987.
Copher, Charles B. "The Bible and the African Experience." Unpublished paper presented to the Pan-African Christian Church Conference, July 19, 1988.
———. "Blacks and Jews in Historical Interaction: The Biblical/African Experience." *The Journal of the Interdenominational Theological Center*, vol. 3, no. 1 (Fall 1975).
———. "The Black Man in the Biblical World." *The Journal of the Interdenominational Theological Center*, vol. 1, no. 2 (Spring 1974).
———. "Egypt and Ethiopia in the Old Testament." *Nile Valley Civilizations*, Ivan Van Sertima, ed. Journal of African Civilizations, Ltd., 1985.
———. "3,000 Years of Biblical Interpretation with Reference to Black Peoples." *The Journal of the Interdenominational Theological Center*, vol. 13, no. 2 (Spring 1986).
Diop, Cheikh Anta. *The African Origins of Civilization: Myth or Reality*. New York: Lawrence Hill, 1974.
———. "Origin of the Ancient Egyptians." *Ancient Civilizations of Africa* (vol. 2 of the UNESCO 8-volume *General History of Africa*), G. Mokhtar, ed. Paris: United Nations Educational, Scientific and Cultural Organization, and University of California Press, 1981.
DuBois, W. E. B. *The World and Africa: An Inquiry into the Part Which Africa Has Played in World History* (New York: Viking Press, 1947).
Eaker, Madeline Hall, ed. *The Heritage of Person County*. Person County, N.C.: The Person County Historical Society in cooperation with Hunter Publishing Company of Winston-Salem, 1981.
Felder, Cain Hope. *Troubling Biblical Waters: Race, Class, and Family*. Maryknoll, N.Y.: Orbis Books, 1989.
Friedrichs, Robert W. *A Sociology of Sociology*. New York/Toronto: Free Press/Collier-Macmillan, 1970, 1972.
Harding, Vincent. *There is a River: The Black Struggle for Freedom in America*. New York: Harcourt Brace Jovanovich, 1981.
Harris, James D., and Edward F. Wente. *X-Ray Atlas of the Royal Mummies*. Chicago: University of Chicago Press, 1980.
Hill, Robert, ed. *Marcus Garvey Universal Negro Improvement Association Papers*, vol. 3. Los Angeles: University of California Press, 1984.
Hopkins, Dwight N. *Black Theology U.S.A. and South Africa: Politics, Culture, and Liberation*. Maryknoll, N.Y.: Orbis Books, 1989.
Issac, Ephraim, and Cain Hope Felder. "The Origins of Ethiopian Civilization." *The Proceedings of the International Conference for Ethiopian Studies*, Addis Ababa, Ethiopia (1985).

James, George G. M. *Stolen Legacy*. San Francisco: Julian Richardson Associates, 1954, 1988.
ben-Jochannan, Yosef A. A. *Africa: Mother of Western Civilization*. Baltimore: Black Classic Press, 1988/New York: Alkebu-lan Books, 1981.
———. *African Origins of the Major Western Religions*. New York: Alkebu-lan Books, 1970.
———. *Black Man of the Nile and His Family*. Baltimore: Black Classic Press, 1989/ New York: Alkebu-lan Books, 1970.
Jones, Major J. *Christian Ethics for Black Theology*. Nashville: Abingdon, 1974.
Leakey, Richard, and Alan Walker. "Homo Erectus Unearthed." *National Geographic*, vol. 168, no. 5 (November 1985).
Muzorewa, Gwinyai. *The Origins and Development of African Theology*. Maryknoll, N.Y.: Orbis Books, 1985.
National Committee of Negro Churchmen. "Black Power Statement." *New York Times* (July 31, 1966).
Rice, Gene. "The African Roots of the Prophet Zephaniah." *The Journal of Religious Thought*, vol. 36, no. 1 (Spring-Summer 1979).
Sertima, Ivan Van. *They Came Before Columbus*. New York: Random House, 1976.
———, ed. *African Presence in Early America*. New Brunswick, N.J.: Transaction Books, 1987.
———, ed. "African Presence in Early Europe." *The Journal of African Civilizations*, vol. 3, no. 1 (1981).
———, ed. *African Presence in Early Europe*. New Brunswick and Oxford: Transaction Books, 1985, 1988).
———, and Runoko Rashidi, eds. "African Presence in Early Asia." *The Journal of African Civilizations*, vol. 7, no. 1, (1988 revised).
———, and Runoko Rashidi, eds. *African Presence in Early Asia*. New Brunswick and Oxford: Transaction Books, 1988.
Wallace, Douglas. "The Search for Adam and Eve." *Newsweek* (January 11, 1988).
Wilmore, Gayraud S. *Black Religion and Black Radicalism: An Interpretation of the Religious History of Afro-American People*. Maryknoll, N.Y.: Orbis Books, 1984.
Wilmore, Gayraud S., and James H. Cone. *Black Theology: A Documentary History, 1966–1979*. Maryknoll, N.Y.: Orbis Books, 1979.
Yates, Walter L. "The God-consciousness of the Black Church in Historical Perspective." *Quest for a Black Theology*, James J. Gardiner and J. Deotis Roberts, eds. Philadelphia: Pilgrim Press, 1971.
Young, Josiah U. *Black and African Theologies: Siblings or Distant Cousins?* Maryknoll, N.Y.: Orbis Books, 1986.

CHAPTER TWO

Freedom as Empowerment

A Black Theological Conception

FREEDOM IN HEBREW AND CHRISTIAN SCRIPTURES

Our appropriation of the philosophy of black power departs from the classic political formulation of this philosophy by Carmichael and Hamilton, and from the prevailing habit of most academic political and social philosophy, in that we do not fail to treat questions about freedom or liberty as, in important respects, religious matters. It has long been the tradition of religious African-Americans to consult the Bible for answers to our questions about the continuing struggle for freedom.

We have learned from Scripture that long before the common era, an African by the name of Moses confronted another African called Pharaoh. What was at issue was the question of freedom—the freedom of an Afro-Asiatic Hebrew people. Through our spirituals we recall that God told Moses to "tell 'ol Pharaoh to let my people go." From our pulpits we have learned that God was not concerned simply that the people be free to go, but more inclusively, that God was concerned that the people might be free to go serve God. In the book of Exodus we are told that Moses was instructed to say to Pharaoh, "the Lord God of the Hebrews hath sent me unto thee, saying, Let my people go, that they may serve me" (Exodus 7:16).

In order to serve more fully the God who favors the cause of freedom, the Hebrew people would need to be emancipated from slavery and oppression, and empowered with opportunity to serve God through building a righteous nation. The liberation agenda of the Exodus-Joshua tradition was animated by a cross-generational covenant between God and Abraham, and relatives and descendants of Abraham. God's covenant with the people of Abraham stipulated that service or obedience to God would contribute to many descendants, a promised land in greater North Africa, the building of a great nation on this land by the many descendants of Abraham, the blessing of other nations through the greatness of this nation; and, negatively, that disobedience would frustrate this agenda. The many descendants, the promised land, and the great and righteous nation that would bless other nations are matters of comprehensive social empowerment, and they are essential to this biblical conception of freedom.

According to the exodus narrative, the ancient Hebrews were emancipated immediately after crossing the Red Sea. The shackles of slavery had been broken. They were emancipated, but not fully free. Between the exodus from Egypt and Joshua's conquest of the promised land, there was the half-freedom of wandering in the wilderness—emancipated but unempowered. They would not be fully free until they had achieved comprehensive social empowerment. Specifically, they would not be fully free until they had come to inhabit a "promised land" in that part of the Afro-Asiatic world we now call greater North Africa where they could build their own righteous nation. The exodus narrative is incomplete without the book of Joshua. Exodus is the act of separation and emancipation, and Joshua is the story of struggle for reformation and comprehensive social empowerment.[1]

"Green is for the land." Regardless of human exploits on and under the sea, in the air, and in outer space, we remain creatures of the land. The right to exist on land is an inalienable human right. A landless people, a people who must inhabit a land in which they cannot be at home, a people who have no access to the wealth and resources of the land, emancipated but unempowered by the land and its fruit, and the opportunity to build a righteous social order, are refugees wandering in the wilderness. It may be that the contemporaries of Moses were correct in perceiving that such unempowered emancipation was hardly to be preferred over slavery in Egypt.[2] We may be emancipated from the shackles of slavery, and from the bondage of apartheid and Jim Crow discrimination, but without access to land and various kinds of wealth and resources, we are not fully free. The God of our ancient African mothers and fathers made the promise of land and access to its wealth an essential part of the ancient Hebrew liberation agenda. It is now an essential part of our liberation agenda.[3]

"Gold is for the wealth." According to the book of Leviticus, to serve the God who favors liberty is to promote access to the land and its resources in a way that serves the interests of all God's people. In this biblical model, access to the land and to wealth is not distributed in strict accordance with individual competition and "free market" or "laissez faire" principles. Leviticus, chapter 25, teaches us that God commanded that each generation observe a year of jubilee. During the year of jubilee, the children of Israel were commanded to "proclaim liberty throughout all the land" (Leviticus 25:10). This divinely prescribed liberty included freedom for those who were enslaved, the cancelation of financial debts, and redistribution of the land such as would ensure that no family was without property. In Leviticus we see explicit recognition of a people's divinely given right to the land and to its wealth. Leviticus offers us a prescriptive vision of a righteous society geared toward the comprehensive social empowerment of all the people. This is divine law. A nation living in obedience to this law is a nation devoted to the comprehensive social empowerment of all the people—and this means land to the people, and food to the people, and wealth to the people, and health care to the people, and housing to the people, and other kinds of wealth and resources and opportunities and power to the people—that is to say, comprehensive social empowerment to all the people.

The New Testament witness to Jesus affirms the same. Those of us who read red-letter editions of the Bible know that in the synoptic Gospels, when one reads the words of Jesus, one is most likely reading about the "kingdom"—the "kingdom of God," or in Matthew "the kingdom of heaven." Jesus preached, above all else, the good news of God's kingdom, and he taught us to pray that "thy kingdom come" and that "thy will be done on earth." God's kingdom, whatever else it may be, is certainly not less than the doing of God's will. That is to say, the kingdom of God is where God reigns, where God's will is done. And it is God's will that the hungry be fed, that the homeless be sheltered, that sick receive care and attention, that the captives be set free. In short, it is God's will that the people be comprehensively empowered—that is, "power to the people." The good news to the poor and the oppressed is that God favors their emancipation and their comprehensive social empowerment. Less than this would fail to be good news to poor and unempowered/oppressed people. To be sure, according to Matthew 25, Jesus teaches us that it is service to God by way of promoting the comprehensive empowerment of the people that separates the sheep from the goats. In God's last judgment, the sheep—the righteous—are those who bring food, shelter, health care, freedom, and opportunity to the people. The goats—the unrighteous—are those who fail to make their contribution to the struggle for comprehensive social empowerment (Matthew 25:31–46).

Many historians and other scholars deny the historical accuracy of these biblical narratives. Many of the events described in Scripture are said never to have actually happened. For instance, it is widely held that the ancient Hebrews never actually observed a year of jubilee. The empirical-historical inerrancy of these narratives is, from our perspective, enormously less significant than what consulting these narratives contributes to our religious self-understanding, and to our understanding of the struggle for freedom. *The philosophy of black power and black theology judge the value of any narrative, philosophy, or account of the world by reference to its liberating answers to our questions about the struggle for freedom.* By this measure, these biblical narratives are of exceedingly great value. Even if, for instance, it could be shown that the ancient Hebrews never observed a year of jubilee, the Leviticus account still offers us a prescriptive vision of righteous socialethical behavior. Likewise, the Exodus-Joshua-Jesus narratives offer us a much fuller conception of freedom than is offered by Pharaoh's or Lincoln's emancipation proclamation.

Emancipation without empowerment is inadequate to the liberation agenda of the Exodus-Joshua tradition. It is inadequate to the New Testament standards of God's kingdom. And it is inadequate to the liberation agenda of modern Africans and African-Americans and landless and unempowered people throughout the world. According to African-American experience, the freedom that comes without comprehensive social empowerment is not true freedom. Such freedom, being reducible to mere emancipation, can be a wandering in the wilderness experience to which, at least to some members of the exodus drama, even slavery might be preferred. Freedom or liberty, rightly conceived, is inclusive of both emancipation and comprehensive social-economic-political empowerment.

MARTIN LUTHER KING, JR.'S, CONCEPTION OF FREEDOM AND THE PHILOSOPHY OF BLACK POWER

Martin Luther King, Jr.'s, conception of freedom is inclusive of comprehensive social-economic-political empowerment. King affirms this point in his book *Where Do We Go From Here: Chaos or Community* when he reflects upon Frederick Douglass's awareness of the inadequacy of emancipation without empowerment:

> With all the beautiful promise that Douglass saw in the Emancipation Proclamation, he soon found that it left the Negro with only abstract freedom. Four million newly liberated slaves found themselves with no bread to eat, no land to cultivate, no shelter to cover their heads. It was like freeing a man who had been unjustly imprisoned for years, and on discovering his innocence sending him out with no bus fare to get home, no suit to cover his body, no financial compensation to atone for his long years of incarceration and to help him get a sound footing in society; sending him out with only the assertion: "Now you are free." What greater injustice could society perpetrate? All the moral voices of the universe, all the codes of sound jurisprudence, would rise up with condemnation at such an act. Yet this is exactly what America did to the Negro. In 1863 the Negro was given abstract freedom expressed in luminous rhetoric. But in an agrarian economy he was given no land to make liberation concrete. After the war the government granted white settlers, without cost, millions of acres of land in the West, thus providing America's new white peasants from Europe with an economic floor. But at the same time its oldest peasantry, the Negro, was denied everything but a legal status he could not use, could not consolidate, could not even defend. As Frederick Douglass came to say, "Emancipation granted the Negro freedom to

hunger, freedom to winter amid the rains of heaven. Emancipation was freedom and famine at the same time." [WDWGFH p. 79]

King saw that freedom without empowerment, without land and other socio-economic resources—that is, mere emancipation—is not true freedom.[4] The freedom that King dreamed of includes comprehensive social empowerment. In this regard, King's dream of freedom is consistent with freedom as conceived by the philosophy of black power. According to the philosophy of black power, and according to King, "let freedom ring" includes "power to the people." And there is yet a more inclusive aspect to King's conception of freedom.

King conceived that the struggle for freedom reaches beyond mere emancipation so as to include struggle for comprehensive social empowerment. Moreover, he understood the struggle to empower the people as an essential part of the struggle to achieve right relationship with God. King gave witness to a conception of freedom that is inclusive of concern for right relation to God when he exclaimed, "Free at last. Free at last. Thank God Almighty, I'm free at last."[5] For King, then, freedom has a profoundly religious character. "Let freedom ring" includes "power to the people" and "get right with God."

Inasmuch as King's conception of freedom includes comprehensive social-political-economic empowerment, King's way of thinking is consistent with the philosophy of black power; but, nonetheless, King expressed "reservations" about the use of "black power" as a slogan (WDWGFH p. 29). King provides us with his reflections upon the use of black power as a slogan in *Where Do We Go From Here*. In the second chapter—entitled "Black Power"—King distinguished between the explicit and correct meaning of black power—its "denotative meaning," and, on the other hand, what the phrase had been mistakenly understood to suggest or imply—its "connotative meaning" (WDWGFH p. 30).

King defined the explicit denotative meaning of black power as "a cry of disappointment" in response "to the failure of white power" (WDWGFH pp. 32–33), "a call to black people to amass the political and economic strength to achieve their legitimate goals" (WDWGFH p. 36), "a call for the pooling of black financial resources to achieve economic security" (WDWGFH p. 38), and as "a psychological call to manhood" (WDWGFH p. 38), which includes a "determination to glory in blackness and to resurrect joyously the African past" (WDWGFH p. 40). And King went on to affirm this understanding of black power:

> No one can deny that the Negro is in dire need of this kind of legitimate power. Indeed, one of the great problems that the Negro confronts is his lack of power. [WDWGFH p. 36]

> To the extent that Black Power advocates these goals, it is a positive and legitimate call to action that we in the civil rights movement have

sought to follow all along and which we must intensify in the future. [WDWGFH p. 38]

King's reservations about the use of black power as a slogan pertain to its connotative meaning, rather than to its denotative meaning. It was King's view that the use of black power as a slogan had inflammatory connotations. In contrast to its explicit denotations, black power brought to mind images of retaliatory violence. Specifically, King found that while "Black Power does not really mean black violence" (WDWGFH p. 54), nonetheless, thanks to the press, and to some loss of faith in the philosophy of nonviolence by many of those who were most ready to appropriate the slogan, black power connoted what it did not really mean. Moreover, King understood that the black power slogan connoted a failure to envision or desire coalitions between blacks and whites (WDWGFH p. 49). Insofar as black power connoted a "separate black path to power and fulfillment that does not intersect white paths" (WDWGFH p. 52), King regarded this as unrealistic. Finally, King found that the slogan had connotations that bespoke "a nihilistic philosophy," which is born of despair and lacks the sustaining power of "the ever-present flame of hope" (WDWGFH pp. 44-46).

King first encountered the use of black power as a slogan when he and SCLC (Southern Christian Leadership Conference) entered into coalition with Stokely Carmichael of SNCC (Student Nonviolent Coordinating Committee) and Floyd McKissick of CORE (Congress of Racial Equality) during the June 1966 James Meredith March against Fear in Mississippi. On this occasion, King, Carmichael, and McKissick had joined together for the purpose of continuing a march that had been interrupted when James Meredith was shot. When the marchers reached Greenwood, Mississippi, Stokely Carmichael and Willie Ricks encouraged the marchers to chant "Black Power!" King identifies the significance of this event for the philosophy of black power by saying:

So Greenwood turned out to be the arena for the birth of the Black Power slogan in the civil rights movement. The phrase had been used long before by Richard Wright and others, but never until that night had it been used as a slogan in the civil rights movement. [WDWGFH p. 29]

In *Where Do We Go From Here* King reports that friction developed between those marchers who wanted "freedom now" as their slogan and those who wanted "black power" as their slogan. Carmichael and McKissick supported the black power slogan. In order to heal this division within the ranks, and also to obviate the negative connotations associated with the "black power" slogan by the press, King successfully persuaded Carmichael, McKissick, and others not to use either slogan for the remainder of the march. This compromise held for the remainder of the march, but it did not prevent "black power" from becoming part of our common nomenclature (WDWGFH pp. 29-32).

Since the 1966 march, black power has grown from being simply a slogan with negative and inflammatory connotations into a fully developed philosophy characterized by its explicit and positive denotations. One of the signal events in the transition from mere slogan with uncertain meaning to a philosophy with explicit and positive denotative meaning was the August 1967 publication of *Black Power: The Politics of Liberation in America* by Stokely Carmichael and Charles V. Hamilton. We may hypothesize that Carmichael learned more than a few things from his work with King during the 1966 march, and on other occasions when they worked together. In any event, *Black Power: The Politics of Liberation in America* is a political philosophy of black power fully consistent with the positive denotations described by King. It is devoid of many of the negative connotations that King objected to when black power was merely a slogan. It is on account of the development of black power's positive denotative meaning by King, and by Carmichael and Hamilton, and by others, that black churchly thought has been able to appropriate a modern philosophy of black power, and thereby produce contemporary black theology.

FREEDOM ACCORDING TO McKISSICK'S PHILOSOPHY OF BLACK NATIONALISM

Let us return to the James Meredith March against Fear in June 1966 where King encounters black power advocacy in the persons of his co-marchers Stokely Carmichael and Floyd McKissick. McKissick's book *Three Fifths of a Man* follows in the tradition of Malcolm X in looking beyond the struggle for domestic U.S. "civil rights" to include concern with international relations and fundamental "human rights." And again, in the tradition of Brother Malcolm, McKissick understands social ethical reflection affirming the human right of African-Americans in the U.S.A. to exercise black power in national and international affairs as a "philosophy of Black Nationalism."[6]

The philosophy of black nationalism understands that we African-Americans in the U.S.A. constitute a distinct nation of people, and that we have a human right to exercise power appropriate to a distinct national population, and that this appropriately includes the exercise of independent black power in international affairs. In *Where Do We Go From Here*, King offers no explicit reflection upon this aspect of black empowerment. But we can be certain that he would have affirmed this human right, because he exercised black power in international affairs by condemning U.S. militarism in Vietnam and elsewhere.[7]

McKissick, who is a constitutional lawyer, points out that the U.S. Declaration of Independence and the U.S. Constitution affirm the inalienable human rights exercised during the American Revolution for independence from Britain. He then goes on to argue that these same documents—when freed of the early white American view that black and colored people are not fully human—that is, "three-fifths of a man"—affirm the exercise of these same human rights by African-Americans struggling for freedom. In other words, an affirmation of the human rights that authorized American nationalism as an essential aspect of Anglo-American freedom is an affirmation that authorizes "Black Nationalism" as an essential aspect of Afro-American freedom. So McKissick maintains that the documents of our American revolutionary constitutional heritage—the U.S. Declaration of Independence and the U.S. Constitution—and "the philosophy of Black Nationalism" are "two essential instruments that, if used together . . . could save America from destruction" (TFM p. 101).

McKissick's articulation of black nationalism, in part because it is articulated in a way that is consistent with American revolutionary nationalism, naturally implies a threat of violence, particularly military violence. From its very beginnings in the Declaration of Independence, American nationalism has presumed an oppressed people's right to have recourse to revolutionary and violent struggle for independence. In subsequent generations we Americans have come to regard perpetual readiness for massive military violence as an unimpeachable national priority. Accordingly, whenever the philosophy of black nationalism is articulated on the model of U.S. American nationalism, it does imply possible recourse to violent struggle for independence.

In *Three Fifths of a Man* McKissick employs the threat of nationalist violence to good effect, but his philosophy of black nationalism is not actually about the business of prescribing African-American violence against whites. To the contrary, McKissick is prescribing social actions that are necessary to avoid a future characterized by increasing violence. The past and present failures of our nation to do justice with regard to the circumstance of African-Americans are creating conditions that rightly entail recourse to anger and to revolutionary violence. In order to prevent our continuing in the direction of increasing violence and destruction, McKissick prescribes comprehensive national black empowerment policies—policies authorized by the U.S. Declaration of Independence and the U.S. Constitution, and by the philosophy of black nationalism.

One of the negative connotations often associated with the philosophy of black nationalism concerns an alleged total unwillingness to enter into coalition efforts with whites. I have already observed that this popular negative connotation is untrue of the philosophy of black power as developed by King in *Where Do We Go From Here*, and now we find that it is equally untrue of the philosophy of black nationalism as developed by McKissick. To be sure, McKissick's main social ethical point is that U.S. public policy communities should join the struggle for black empowerment by exercising the authority of the U.S. Declaration of Independence and the U.S. Constitution in ways that favor the independence and empowerment of African-American and other people. McKissick explicitly calls upon the president, the courts, the legislature, the legal profession, lawyers, and law schools to become social engineers and agents for progress (TFM pp. 85, 90). McKissick says, "Proper use of the Constitution can be a way to put the full power and resources of the national government into the drive to gain freedom—the drive to achieve Black Power" (TFM p. 55). In that McKissick's aim is to convince the U.S. public policy community, especially the judiciary, to join the struggle for the empowerment of a black nation, there is no good reason to accept the view that black nationalist philosophy rules out cooperative and coalition efforts with whites and others who wish to contribute to the cause of freedom and empowerment.

The philosophy of black nationalism as expressed by McKissick—and as is consistent with a nonracist version of American nationalism, and as is consistent with the black nationalist philosophy of Malcolm X—conceives of freedom in such a way as to insist upon the fundamental human right of distinct nations of people—including African-Americans in the U.S.A., native Americans, Palestinians, black South Africans, and others—to exercise the independence, liberty, and power appropriate to any nation. And this includes the kinds of environmental and economic resources (including land) appropriate to any nation.[8]

McKissick's reflection upon the philosophy of black nationalism from the angle of U.S. constitutional law is no more theologically reflective than the U.S. Declaration of Independence and the U.S. Constitution. But he does draw upon sources that are more theologically reflective. For instance, McKissick points us to David Walker's 1829 booklet—"Walker's Appeal, in Four Articles, Together with a Preamble, to the Colored Citizens of the World but in Particular, and Very Expressly to Those of the United States" (TFM pp. 111–13). David Walker's appeal on behalf of freedom for African-American slaves, and his description of the African-American circumstance, is woven through and through with explicit reflection upon God's place in our history. McKissick also makes appeal to Richard Allen (founder of the African Methodist Episcopal Church) and to Allen's praise for David Walker's appeal (TFM pp. 112ff.). Furthermore, McKissick points to the Reverend Henry Highland Garnet as "an early advocate of Black Power" (TFM p. 117), to the inspiring legacy of Nat Turner (TFM pp. 114–15), and to other African-American preachers and church leaders who nurtured a sense of common black national identity among Africans in the New World (TFM pp. 111–15).[9] And of course we know that the black nationalist thought of Malcolm X is a deeply religious inheritance.

McKissick's appeal to theologically reflective sources and to religious and church leaders is more than incidental. For one thing, as Gayraud Wilmore teaches us in *Black Religion and Black Radicalism*, it is a historical fact that black power and black nationalist philosophies have considerable rootage in African-American religion. It is, then, to be expected that a historically conscious philosophy of black nationalism would appeal to its

African-American religious heritage. Furthermore, conceptually, the idea that the freedom and empowerment of our people rightly includes the development of a separate and independently empowered black nation is very little removed from our churchly tradition of black separatist movements leading to the establishment of independent black churches and denominations.

THE STRUGGLE CONTINUES

While James Meredith was in the hospital recovering from gunshot wounds, his march against fear continued under the coalition leadership of the Reverend Dr. Martin Luther King, Jr., attorney Floyd McKissick, and brother Stokely Carmichael. We know from King's account that it was sometimes difficult to keep this coalition together. By taking King to represent the social ethical view of African-American Christianity, Carmichael to represent black power advocacy, and McKissick to represent black nationalist thought, we learn that these diverse lines of thought can hold together. Despite their differences, the King-Carmichael-McKissick coalition held throughout the march. Black Christianity had worked effectively, but uneasily, with black power and black nationalist thought.

The uneasiness was caused, in large part, by false implications, connotations, and sensational exaggerations. King and others were mindful of the fact that at that time many people wrongly understood black power and black nationalist thought in terms of black racism, an absolute condemnation of all white people that prohibited coalition and reconciliation, and even in terms of genocide against white people. By the end of the 1966 march it was obvious that the philosophy of black power was badly in need of clarification. After the march, each of the three published a clear denotative account of the philosophy of black power: King in 1967 with his chapter entitled "Black Power" in *Where Do We Go From Here*; Carmichael, and Charles V. Hamilton, in 1967 with *Black Power: The Politics of Liberation in America*; and McKissick in 1969 with *Three Fifths of a Man*.

The resources provided by King, Carmichael and Hamilton, and McKissick are valuable contributions to the clarification of the positive denotative meaning of the philosophy of black power. During the 1966 march, the King-Carmichael-McKissick coalition held because, between them and their common commitment to the struggle for comprehensive political and socio-economic empowerment, there was more agreement than disagreement. Now that each of them has contributed to the development of a carefully considered philosophy of black power, we are better prepared to continue our march toward freedom and empowerment.[10]

This second chapter—"Freedom as Empowerment"—could as well have been entitled "Liberty as Empowerment" because our conception of liberty, like our conception of freedom, includes comprehensive social-economic-political and religious empowerment. Just as too often freedom is inadequately conceived, so too there are conceptions of liberty that are not adequately inclusive of comprehensive empowerment. But, as we use the language, freedom and liberty are equivalent concepts, and accordingly, both include comprehensive empowerment.

In many of our communities, and in other Third World communities where freedom/liberty is thought to include comprehensive social-economic-political empowerment, the social process of striving or struggling or fighting to achieve freedom/liberty is spoken of in terms of liberation or liberation struggle. Our struggle for liberty or freedom does not end with simple emancipation, and it does not end with voting rights and civil rights. Our liberation struggle includes struggle for comprehensive social-economic-political and religious empowerment. According to black theology, contribution to the struggle for comprehensive social empowerment is essential to any quest for right relationship to God. As we learn from consulting Matthew 25, in God's final judgment, service to the struggle for freedom and empowerment counts as service to God, and failure to serve this cause counts as failure to serve God.[11] Black theology is, then, consistent with the traditions of the black church revolution, and consistent with early Afro-Asiatic Hebrew and Christian conceptions of freedom, when it, like Martin Luther King, Jr., appropriates black power's and black nationalism's conception of freedom/liberty as inclusive of comprehensive social-economic-political empowerment, and when it does so in a way that is ever mindful of right relationship to God. Again, "let freedom ring" includes "power to the people" and "get right with God."[12]

NOTES

1. I was very much helped in thinking through the Exodus-Joshua relationship to emancipation and empowerment by conversations with Dr. Cleveland Gay—one of the leading members of St. Luke "Community" United Methodist Church (Zan W. Holmes, pastor) in Dallas, Texas.

2. "And the children of Israel said unto them, would to God we had died by the hand of the Lord in the land of Egypt, when we sat by the flesh pots, and when we did eat bread to the full; for ye have brought us forth into this wilderness, to kill this whole assembly with hunger" (Exodus 16:3). In this narrative, the children of Israel are complaining to Moses and Aaron about their status as wanderers in the wilderness after their emancipation from slavery in Egypt. They regard starving in the wilderness as worse than slavery in Egypt. But of course, as the story goes, they did not starve in the wilderness, and the next generation was empowered by Joshua's conquest and occupation of the promised land.

3. In *There is a River: The Black Struggle for Freedom in America* (New York: Harcourt Brace Jovanovich, 1981), Vincent Harding points to historical examples of African-American conceptions of freedom from the 1860s, which included a desire for land (pp. 255, 264–65). Harding makes it clear that African-Americans have long conceived that without land, freedom is incomplete. Also, Harding teaches us that an adequate reflection upon African-American claims to land in

the New World must include serious attention to the prior claims of those who were here before us—the indigenous peoples who are collectively called Native Americans or, less appropriately, American Indians (p. 63). Moreover, attention to a Native American perspective, such as that forwarded by Robert Allen Warrior, challenges us to admit the extent to which our interpretation of the Exodus-Joshua traditions in terms of emancipation-empowerment depends upon our failure to attend more empathically to the plight and rights of the prior inhabitants of the promised land—the Canaanites. The perspective of indigenous peoples—like Native Americans, black South Africans, Palestinians, and other traditional peoples who have suffered at the hands of foreign invaders who held that God had chosen them to be the new rulers of the land—should warn us that the Exodus-Joshua traditions can and have been put to unrighteous and counter-liberating purposes. Robert Allen Warrior's "Canaanites, Cowboys, and Indians: Deliverance, Conquest, and Liberation Theology Today" in *Christianity and Crisis* (September 11, 1989), challenges us to correct abuses of the Exodus-Joshua traditions by putting the Canaanites "at the center of Christian theological reflection," and Warrior says, "They are the last remaining ignored voice in the text, except perhaps for the land itself" (p. 264).

4. Similarly, in "Of the Dawn of Freedom"—the second chapter of *The Souls of Black Folk* (Nashville: Fisk University Press, 1979)—and in *Black Reconstruction in America 1860–1880* (New York: S.A. Russell, 1935), W. E. B. DuBois recognizes that freedom without empowerment (inclusive of land) is inadequate, and therefore he laments the failure of the post–Civil War reconstruction efforts—specifically those of the Freedmen's Bureau—to empower the newly emancipated slaves. Also, for an extended account of the failure of U.S. post–Civil War reconstruction efforts to empower newly emancipated African-Americans with land and other socio-economic resources, see Clause F. Oubre, *Forty Acres and a Mule: The Freedmen's Bureau and Black Land Ownership* (Baton Rouge: Louisiana State University Press, 1978) and Edward Magdol, *A Right to the Land: Essays on the Freedmen's Community* (Westport, Conn.: Greenwood Press, 1977).

5. I am indebted to Professor Schubert Ogden, my colleague at the Perkins School of Theology, for pointing my attention to "Free at Last" as an example of King's religious conception of freedom.

6. In *The Autobiography of Malcolm X*, Alex Haley, ed. (New York: Ballantine Books, 1973), Malcolm X says "that the struggle of the American black man is international." He describes the struggle as a struggle not only for "civil rights," but also, and more fundamentally, as a struggle for "human rights" (p. 364). He argues for a philosophy of "black nationalism," and he acknowledges the influence of Marcus Garvey (p. 374).

7. In "Black American Demands" in *Foreign Policy* (Fall 1985), Kenneth Longmyer points to King's opposition to U.S. militarism in Vietnam and to the Free South Africa Movement as examples of African-American attempts to influence U.S. foreign policy, but he finds that African-American involvement in foreign policy formulation is "very limited" (p. 11). Longmyer goes on to report that most African-Americans in the U.S.A. agree that we should reduce defense spending, reduce U.S. military intervention abroad, be more sympathetic to Palestinians, to Third World needs, and to the United Nations (pp. 12–14). He expresses approval of African-American efforts to exercise power in international affairs.

8. The philosophy of black nationalism affirms that every nation is entitled to

a national liberty that includes land and other socio-economic resources for its people. Similarly, our liberation colors symbolize our awareness that liberty or freedom includes equal access to land—"green is for the land"—and to other socio-economic resources—"gold is for the wealth." Accordingly, our liberation flag is properly identified as a symbol for black nationalism. That it is proper to take our liberation flag (the most popular symbol of black power advocacy in the U.S.A.) to be a symbol of black nationalism is verified in the historical fact that Marcus Garvey's UNIA established the colors red-black-green as "national colors." See Robert Hill, ed., *Marcus Garvey Universal Negro Improvement Association Papers*, volume 3 (Los Angeles: University of California Press, 1984), pp. 318–19.

9. The reader may care to consult Henry Highland Garnet's 1843 "Address to the Slaves of the United States of America." The Reverend Garnet's address and David Walker's "Appeal," along with Garnet's brief sketch of Walker's life, and a brief introduction by William Loren Katz appear in *The American Negro: His History and Literature* (New York: Arno Press and the *New York Times*, 1969).

10. For an extended account of an African-American Christian appropriation of the black nationalist aspects of the philosophy of black power, see the Reverend Albert B. Cleage, *Black Christian Nationalism: New Directions for the Black Church* (New York: William Morrow, 1972). For reflection upon Marcus Garvey's pioneering influence upon black power and black nationalist thought, see Theodore G. Vincent, *Black Power and the Garvey Movement* (Berkeley, Calif.: Ramparts Press, 1971). The student of African-American Muslim appropriations of black nationalist thought should be certain to consult the thinking of the Honorable Elijah Mohammed, Malcolm X, Wallace Dean Mohammed, and Minister Louis Farrakhan.

11. This understanding of Matthew 25 is very much informed by the preaching of the Reverend Theodore Walker, Sr. During his eighteen years of service as pastor of First Calvary Baptist Church in Salisbury, North Carolina, he regularly preached about the necessary connection between service to God and service to others. In one such sermon, entitled "Getting Right With God," he taught us that "the way we go about getting right with God is by first getting right with our neighbors" (see Matthew 25:23-24).

12. The connection between struggle for freedom and right relationship to God is affirmed by D. Kortright Davis, "Emancipatory Theology as Doxology: Freedom Sings What Freedom Brings" in *The Journal of Religious Thought*, vol. 45, no. 1 (Summer-Fall 1988). Here Davis develops an expanded conception of emancipation—a conception that goes beyond the simple emancipation proclaimed by "the British Parliament, or Abraham Lincoln, or P. W. Botha" (p. 34). Davis develops an emancipatory theology in which doxology or glorification of God necessarily includes contribution to the struggle for justice (pp. 41–42). From Davis we learn that in order for theology to praise God rightly, it must contribute to the struggle for freedom and empowerment.

BIBLIOGRAPHY

Carmichael, Stokely, and Charles V. Hamilton. *Black Power: The Politics of Liberation in America*. New York: Vintage Books, 1967.

Cleage, Albert B. *Black Christian Nationalism: New Directions for the Black Church*. New York: William Morrow, 1972.

Davis, D. Kortright. "Emancipatory Theology as Doxology: Freedom Sings What Freedom Brings." *The Journal of Religious Thought*, vol. 45, no. 1 (Summer-Fall 1988).

DuBois, W. E. B. *Black Reconstruction in America 1860–1880*. New York: S. A. Russell, 1935.

———. *The Souls of Black Folk*. Nashville: Fisk University Press, 1979.

Garnet, Henry Highland. "Address to the Slaves of the United States of America (1843)." *The American Negro: His History and Literature*. New York: Arno Press and the New York Times, 1969.

Harding, Vincent. *There is a River: The Black Struggle for Freedom in America*. New York: Harcourt Brace Jovanovich, 1981.

Hill, Robert, ed. *Marcus Garvey Universal Negro Improvement Association Papers*, vol. 3. Los Angeles: University of California Press, 1984.

King, Jr., Martin Luther. *Where Do We Go From Here: Chaos or Community*. New York: Harper and Row, 1967.

Longmyer, Kenneth. "Black American Demands." *Foreign Policy* (Fall 1985).

Magdol, Edward. *A Right to the Land: Essays on the Freedmen's Community*. Westport, Conn.: Greenwood Press, 1977.

McKissick, Floyd. *Three Fifths of a Man*. Toronto: Macmillan, 1969.

Oubre, Clause F. *Forty Acres and a Mule: The Freedmen's Bureau and Black Land Ownership*. Baton Rouge: Louisiana State University Press, 1978.

Vincent, Theodore G. *Black Power and the Garvey Movement*. Berkeley: Ramparts Press, 1971.

Walker, David. "Walker's Appeal, in Four Articles, Together with a Preamble, to the Colored Citizens of the World but in Particular, and Very Expressly to Those of the United States (1829)." *The American Negro: His History and Literature*. New York: Arno Press and the New York Times, 1969.

Warrior, Robert Allen. "Canaanites, Cowboys, and Indians: Deliverance, Conquest, and Liberation Theology Today." *Christianity and Crisis* (Sept. 11, 1989).

Wilmore, Gayraud. *Black Religion and Black Radicalism: An Interpretation of the Religious History of Afro-American People*. Maryknoll, N.Y.: Orbis Books, 1973, 1984.

X, Malcolm. *The Autobiography of Malcolm X*, Alex Haley, ed. New York: Ballantine Books, 1964, 1973.

CHAPTER THREE

The Ethic of Breaking Bread

Sociological Descriptions, Predictions, and Socio-Ethical Prescriptions for Liberal Coalition Efforts

LET US BREAK BREAD TOGETHER

It is typical of African-American Christianity to conceive of "righteousness," or right relation to God, in social and ethical terms. In our churches we like to speak, to sing, to pray, and to preach about getting right with God. And we understand that to "get right with God" is to do God's will. According to Scripture, it is God's will that we provide adequate food, shelter, clothing, health care, liberty, and other resources and opportunity for all the people (see Matthew 25). In this sense, "get right with God" entails "power to the people"—that is to say, in order to achieve right relationship to God, we must contribute to the empowerment of the people.

This social ethical or horizontal dimension of right relationship to God is profoundly expressed at our communion tables. At the sacrament of holy communion, we give witness to our voluntary association with the long tradition of Christian communities which perceive that the breaking of bread is at the very heart and soul of right relationship to God.

For us, bread is an inclusive symbol. Our social location enables us to be certain that when the early followers of Jesus prayed "give us this day our daily bread," never did they conceive of bread in such a way as to fail to include "bread"—that is, food and other basic nourishment. Jesus spoke to a social location where serious hunger and starvation were clear and present realities. This literal sense of bread as food—physical nourishment—is not lost in our prayer for daily bread. But in addition to this, we understand bread to symbolize other necessities. Bread is a symbol for food, for money, for wealth, and for other resources and opportunities. Comprehensively conceived, to break bread means to share food and money and land and power and other resources, including spiritual and religious resources, with the people.

The symbol of breaking bread, then, provides us with a model, and a counter-model, for social behavior: the ethic of breaking bread, and the ethic of crumbs.

The Ethic of Crumbs

In the Gospel of Luke, chapter 16:19ff., we read: "There was a certain rich man, which was clothed in purple and fine linen, and fared sumptuously every day. And there was a certain beggar named Lazarus, which was laid at his gate, full of sores. And desiring to be fed with the crumbs which fell from the rich man's table...." In the following verses, we are told that the rich man died and went to hell.

What was the rich man's offense? It was not simply, if at all, that he was an unbeliever. The rich man went to hell because he refused to share. He refused to break bread with his neighbor Lazarus. The rich man failed to meet the standard of righteousness that distinguishes the sheep from the goats in Matthew 25. The goats are those who fail to serve God by breaking bread with the neighbor. The rich man was one of these.

The rich man is a symbol for those of us who refuse to break bread with the people. Too often, we are like this rich man who, rather than breaking bread with those in need, preferred that the poor feed upon the crumbs that "trickle down" from the well-supplied side of the economy. Too often we say, "Let the poor have our leftovers. Let the poor eat crumbs. If they haven't enough to eat, then we will have to have bigger and more sumptuous feasts (increased profits to stimulate investments) so as to generate a larger trickle of crumbs." This is "trickle-down" or "supply-side" ethics. This is the ethics of the rich man who went to hell. This is the ethics of unrighteousness. This is the ethic of crumbs.

The Ethic of Breaking Bread

When at holy communion we sing and pray "let us break bread together on our knees," we are not praying for an increased trickle of crumbs. We are praying for a relationship to God that compels us to do righteousness; that is, we are praying for a relationship to God that compels us to contribute to the empowerment of the people through sharing bread rather than crumbs.

At Shiloh Baptist Church in Greensboro, North Carolina, our pastor, the Reverend Otis Hairston, habitually concludes communion and other services with an admonishment to the effect that "the church is not contained within the brick walls of this edifice; instead, the church is where God's will is done in the world. What we do here is to equip ourselves to do righteousness." The Reverend Hairston describes Shiloh as an "equipping station" where we are enabled and empowered to go forth and be the church in the world. Some of us speak of such empowerment in terms of the movement of the holy spirit.[1] On the first Sunday of each month, we break bread at the communion table inside the sanctuary so as to instruct ourselves about how God would have us behave throughout the week outside the sanctuary.

Here this instruction is called "the ethic of breaking bread." Our study of Hebrew and Christian Scriptures indicates that the ethic of breaking bread is a divinely given imperative. Individually and collectively we are called to contribute to the increase of righteousness; that is, we are called to break such bread as contributes to the comprehensive social empowerment of the people.

Comprehensively conceived, breaking bread is as much about politics, economics, and other social activity as it is about the religion of individuals at the communion table. Righteousness is doing God's will, and it is God's will that we break bread with the people. Moreover, the ethic of breaking bread is prescribed not only for the rich who have a surplus of bread, and whose cup runneth over, it is also prescribed for those of us who have only a little. In the story of the feeding of the five thousand (Matthew 14:13–21, Mark 6:30–44, Luke 9:10–17, John 6:1–14), Jesus calls upon those of us who have only a little fish and a few loaves to share even that little bit. All of us, rich and poor alike, are called to the ethic of breaking bread.

When at the communion table we sing and pray, "let us break bread together on our knees," we are at the same time praying for right relationship to God. And we understand that in order for us to "get right with God," we must seek to "empower the people" through the ethic of breaking bread.

THE AFRICAN-AMERICAN CIRCUMSTANCE IN THE 1980s AND LIBERAL PUBLIC POLICY PRESCRIPTIONS FOR THE 1990s

There is a long tradition of North American political thought, going back to John Locke, Adam Smith, and John Stuart Mill, called "liberalism" or liberal political theory. North American liberalism understands freedom to be about the liberty of individuals to pursue their chosen interests, particularly in the area of economic gain. This traditional North American political thought has developed along two lines, which today are commonly called "liberal" and "conservative." Today's liberalism and conservatism are, then, two strands growing from a traditional American liberalism that emphasizes freedom to pursue individual interests. The liberalism of today is distinguished from the conservative strand of traditional North American liberalism by its conviction that public or governmental and other sectors of society should go beyond the conservative public policy agenda (protecting the right of individuals to do whatever they individually choose to do) so as to include efforts to ensure the social well-being of all members of society.

In some current varieties of liberalism this more inclusive public policy agenda is informed by a more inclusive conception of freedom. For example, Franklin I. Gamwell in *Beyond Preference: Liberal Theories of Independent Associations* describes the difference between, on the one hand, a "reformed liberalism," which is indebted to John Dewey's "new individualism," and, on the other hand, forms of liberal political thought where freedom or liberty is less inclusively conceived, by saying, "in the 'new individualism,' liberty is not the freedom from restraint to pursue economic benefits, but the freedom so to interact with others as to make a distinctive contribution to them, the opportunity to associate democratically" (BPLT p. 108). Reformed liberalism is, then, informed by a conception of freedom that reaches beyond protection of individual freedom or preference so as to include regard for community and public well-being.

Modern liberalism in general holds that public/governmental and other sectors of society should aspire not only to protect individual freedoms of choice, but also that these sectors should contribute positively to the well-being of all members of society. Such liberalism—on account of its more inclusive conception of freedom, and correspondingly, on account of its call for public and other sectors of society to contribute to the increase of freedom and well-being for all—is a form of social and political thought more in agreement with our black churchly understanding of freedom, and more in agreement with our churchly ethic of breaking bread, than conservative forms of North American liberalism, which deny that the public sector (particularly federal government) is morally obliged to make breadbreaking and empowering contributions to the well-being of merely emancipated people.

The characteristic liberal conviction that public and other sectors of society should develop comprehensive and affirmative (not merely trickle-down) policies aimed at contributing to the optimal well-being of all, including in particular those suffering from poverty and related socio-economic disadvantage, is a secular and political view consistent with the ethic of breaking bread. *The purpose of this chapter is to present liberal sociological views from the 1980s of the African-American circumstance and, prescriptively, of the bread that public and other sectors of U.S. society should break to improve upon this circumstance in the 1990s and beyond.* In the next chapter we shall engage in critical evaluation of particular aspects of these liberal views from the churchly perspective of black theology.

I noted in chapter 1 that Carmichael and Hamilton's work in political science has explicit social ethical content. Their work includes social ethical prescriptions aimed at contributing to "the cause" of freedom or liberty. And here liberty is understood to include the comprehensive social-political-economic empowerment of all the people. Carmichael and Hamilton treat mainly the explicitly political aspects of African-American social empowerment. We turn now from the political science of Carmichael and Hamilton to consider work in another wing of the social science academy—sociology and public policy. Sociology and public policy, being social scientific macroscopic descriptions, predictions, and associated public policy prescriptions or recommendations, is also a social ethical endeavor.

William Julius Wilson is professor of sociology and public policy at the University of Chicago and the 1989 president of the American Sociology Association. Wilson's work in sociology and public policy has an explicitly prescriptive component like that of Carmichael and Hamilton in being concerned with contributing to freedom from poverty and related forms of deprivation. Typologically, a major difference is that Wilson is addressing his social ethical prescriptions to public policy communities while Carmichael and Hamilton are writing social ethical prescriptions for the black community. That is to say, Carmichael and Hamilton are concerned with prescribing ways to employ the socio-political power of African-American communities in solving macroscopic social problems, while Wilson is concerned with prescribing ways to employ the socio-economic power of U.S. public policy communities in solving macroscopic social problems. Wilson's work is addressed to liberal and social democratic public policy-makers. Carmichael and Hamilton address themselves to African-Americans (political activists in particular) within disadvantaged communities. Thus, while Wilson, Carmichael, and Hamilton are all African-Americans working in secular social science and social ethics to empower the people, Wilson's work, because it is not concerned primarily with exercising the liberating power of black communities, is not, strictly speaking, classified under the category of black power.

Given that Wilson's work falls outside the category of black power, and given that Wilson is as neglectful of relationship to God as Carmichael and Hamilton (and nearly all academic social science), it might seem that his work is more than a little beyond the immediate interest of black theology's attempt to do social ethics in a way that is consistent with the religious tradition of the black church revolution and the philosophy of black power. But this is not the case, because both the liberating aims of the philosophy of black power and the universality of the Christian call for righteousness require that our social ethical reflections include concern with cross-cultural dialogue and with coalition and ecumenical efforts to empower all the people through the ethic of breaking bread.[2]

The philosophy of black power as articulated by Carmichael and Hamilton admits the desirability of liberating coalition efforts. But they stipulate that meaningful coalitions presuppose, among other things, the existence of an independent base of power that "does not depend for ultimate decision-making on a force outside itself" (BP p. 79).[3] In regard to electoral politics specifically, Carmichael and Hamilton hold that African-Americans in the U.S.A. must cease being so dependent upon the ups and downs of predominantly Anglo-American Democratic and Republican parties (BP p.

42). Our goal should not be simply to integrate and assimilate ourselves into predominantly white political parties. They observe that those few of us who are assimilated into predominantly white political parties are largely unable to contribute much to improving conditions for all (BP pp. 53–54). Rather than striving simply for political integration and assimilation, they prescribe that African-Americans in the U.S.A. should form "new political structures" and racially separated and relatively independently empowered institutions of various kinds (BP pp. 86, 144, 166). For Carmichael and Hamilton, in political and other realms of macroscopic social existence, independent black power is an essential precondition for meaningful and liberating coalition efforts (see chapter 3—"The Myth of Coalition").

In the ecclesial world, the condition that admits the possibility of meaningful and liberating coalition efforts actually exists in the form of racially separate and independently empowered African-American denominations and churches. We have already achieved in the congregational-religious sphere of life what Carmichael and Hamilton say we need to achieve in political, economic, and other social spheres of life. Moreover, the history of the black church's involvement in abolitionist, civil rights, human rights, and peace movements is evidence of its willingness to engage in liberating coalition efforts.[4] Also, black churches have readily engaged in ecumenical dialogues and movements, but always in accordance with a desire to preserve their status as racially separate and independently empowered and controlled institutions. This is to say, the coalition and ecumenical efforts of the black churches have been, in fact, conducted in accordance with the preconditions stipulated by the philosophy of black power.

Thus, the philosophy of black power and its elder tradition of racially separated and independently empowered African-American churches affirm the desirability of liberating coalitions to empower the people through the ethic of breaking bread. In our churches at least we have achieved the kind of independence that is, according to Carmichael and Hamilton, prerequisite to genuinely liberating coalition efforts. Accordingly, social ethical reflection for public policy and other communities is not beyond our interest. Given the struggle for and achievement of conditions that permit the possibility of liberating coalition efforts, the formulation of a coalition agenda can be an important part of black power's and black theology's social ethical reflection. Black theological social ethics is, then, justifiably interested in William Julius Wilson's liberal views and social ethical prescriptions for public policy communities.

The Truly Disadvantaged

In 1978 Wilson described the social circumstance of African-Americans in the U.S.A. in terms of "the worsening condition of the black underclass" and "the improving condition of the black middle class"—*The Declining Significance of Race*. In 1987 Wilson published *The Truly Disadvantaged: The*

Inner City, the Underclass, and Public Policy. In this book Wilson goes beyond socio-scientific description to include explicit public policy recommendations. (And thus, social science engages in normative social ethical reflection.) Wilson's public policy recommendations aim to "ameliorate inner-city social conditions," which typify "the worsening conditions of the black underclass" in the United States (TD p. viii).

The first part of *The Truly Disadvantaged* — "The Ghetto Underclass, Poverty, and Social Dislocation" — is a socio-scientific description of the worsening circumstances of a growing inner city underclass in which African-Americans are disproportionately represented. Inner city poverty is associated with what Wilson calls "social dislocations." Wilson's work — like that of earlier social-scientific descriptions by Kenneth B. Clark, E. Franklin Frazier, Bayard Rustin, Daniel Moynihan, and others — emphasizes such social dislocations as, first and foremost, the deterioration of African-American families in the U.S.A.; and contributing or related social dislocations, which include "urban blacks' rising rates of broken marriages, female-headed homes, out-of-wedlock births, welfare dependency," and unemployment (TD pp. 20–21). Moynihan's famous study drew attention to the problems of social dislocation and black family deterioration in 1965, but since then these problems have gotten much worse.[5] They have, according to Wilson, "reached catastrophic proportions" (TD p. 21):

> To be more specific, one quarter of all black births occurred outside of marriage in 1965, the year Moynihan wrote his report on the Negro family, and by 1980 57 percent were; in 1965 nearly 25 percent of all black families were headed by women, and by 1980 43 percent were; partly as a result, welfare dependency among poor blacks has mushroomed. And perhaps the most dramatic indicator of the extent to which social dislocations have afflicted urban blacks is crime, especially violent crime, which has increased sharply in recent years. Finally, these growing social problems have accompanied increasing black rates of joblessness. [TD p. 21]

The dramatic difference between the very bad circumstance faced by the inner city underclass (among whom African-Americans are disproportionately represented) in 1965 and the very much worse circumstance that obtained in the 1980s indicates that it is justifiable for Wilson to speak in terms of "catastrophic proportions."

The second part of *The Truly Disadvantaged* — "The Ghetto Underclass and Public Policy" — advances public policy prescriptions or recommendations designed to "improve the life chances of truly disadvantaged groups" (TD p. x). Wilson's own public policy recommendations are preceded by an analysis of previous failed and inadequate public policy efforts. Race-specific policies, race relations approaches, and the war on poverty are public policy approaches that failed to improve the worsening condition of the African-American underclass. Such policies are said to have failed because they did not address socio-economic-labor-market societal arrangements, which are more significant in determining the life chances of underclass African-Americans than is presentday racism. While not surrendering the need for race-specific policies such as affirmative action (policies that have benefited middle-class African-Americans, but which have largely failed to improve the life chances of inner city underclass African-Americans), Wilson perceives that in order to benefit the African-American inner city underclass, we must "relate the problems of minority poverty directly to the broader problems of economic organization" (TD p. ix). Accordingly, Wilson prescribes:

> The problems of the ghetto underclass can be most meaningfully addressed by a comprehensive program that combines employment policies with social welfare policies and that features universal as opposed to race- or group-specific strategies. On the one hand, this program highlights macroeconomic policy to generate a tight labor market and economic growth; fiscal and monetary policy not only to stimulate noninflationary growth, but also to increase the competitiveness of American goods on both the domestic and international markets; and a national labor-market strategy to make the labor force more adaptable to changing economic opportunities. On the other hand, this program highlights a child support assurance program, a family allowance program, and a child care strategy. [TD p. 163]

Here we see that in addition to recommending a comprehensive public policy agenda that includes fiscal and inflation-checking monetary policies designed to create economic growth, a tight labor market (full employment), and other changes in the urban economy, Wilson also offers a "political strategy" (TD p. 164) or public relations advice about how to push for such policy. Not only must we get beyond race-specific policies to reach truly disadvantaged African-Americans, but we must also get beyond pushing such policies as race-specific or class-specific platforms. Wilson "advances a social democratic public-policy agenda designed to improve the life chances of truly disadvantaged groups such as the ghetto underclass by emphasizing programs to which the more advantaged groups of all races can positively relate" (TD p. viii). Wilson says that "the hidden agenda for liberal policymakers is to enhance the chances in life for the ghetto underclass by emphasizing programs to which the more advantaged groups of all class and racial backgrounds can positively relate" (TD p. 163). In order to sell or market Wilson's social democratic public policy, the emphasis must be upon the way in which it benefits all people, rather than upon its "hidden agenda" that is benefiting the truly disadvantaged.

Recalling Bayard Rustin's plea from the early 1960s for a "broad-based political coalition" to achieve "fundamental economic reform," Wilson prescribes "a progressive reform coalition" (TD p. 155). The social ethical implication of Wilson's analysis for black churches and other parts of the black community is that, if our aim is to benefit the truly disadvantaged, we should seek to contribute to the actualization of this liberal social democratic agenda. We should engage in coalition and ecumenical efforts to generate policies designed to achieve the kinds of comprehensive changes required to benefit the truly disadvantaged. Moreover, taking account of Wilson's political strategy for broad-based progressive coalition building, we should emphasize the benefits that will obtain for all U.S. citizens rather than emphasizing the benefits that will obtain for those who are truly disadvantaged.

This last imperative is important advice for building broad-based coalitions. Indeed, Carmichael and Hamilton hold that a clear understanding of what benefits will obtain for all parties is a necessary precondition for successful coalition efforts (BP pp. 79–80). The philosophy of black power, then, agrees with Wilson in understanding that successful coalition efforts must include emphasis upon how others stand to benefit from contributing to the cause of freedom and comprehensive social empowerment.

The State of Black America

Another major scholarly work in sociology and public policy that presents to U.S. public policy communities a social ethical coalition agenda for improving the circumstance of disadvantaged people in the U.S.A. is the National Urban League's 1989 report—*The State of Black America 1989*. Like Wilson, the Urban League's social ethic is "liberal" in that it shares the characteristic liberal conviction that public and other sectors of society should develop comprehensive and affirmative (not merely trickle-down) policies aimed at improving the status of disadvantaged people.

Perhaps the most striking difference between the social ethical prescriptions offered by the National Urban League and those offered by Wilson is in the area of political strategy. The Urban League adopts an alternative to Wilson's hidden-agenda approach. Rather than avoiding race-specific descriptions of the problems of poverty and social disadvantage, and avoiding emphasis upon benefits for disadvantaged African-Americans, the Urban League describes the African-American circumstance in terms of a growing economic gap or inequality between blacks and whites. It prescribes a public policy designed to narrow and close this gap by the year 2000. "Parity 2000" is the Urban League's name for a proposed massive public and private sector effort to bring black people in the U.S.A. into economic parity with whites by the end of this century.

In the opening essay of the Urban League's 1989 report, the president and C.E.O., John E. Jacob, prescribes a national coalition effort—including the private sector, the black community, and government, especially the federal government—to achieve economic parity between blacks and whites in the United States. Jacob would like to see the economic gap between blacks and whites closed at a rate of "seven percent a year between now and 2000." He appeals to the Bush administration to articulate the goal of parity by 2000, and to implement specific programs designed to meet that end (SBA/89 p. 5). "Government," says Jacob, "has to be the prime mover of such a national effort for only it has the power and the resources to implement nationwide programs that have an impact, and only it has the moral and constitutional leadership role that can marshall private and non-profit groups behind national objectives" (SBA/89 p. 5). Jacob announces the Urban League's intention "to press our Parity 2000 goal upon the new administration and the Congress and to enlist public support for it" (SBA/89 p. 6).

While Parity 2000 focuses mainly upon the economic disadvantage of African-Americans in the U.S.A., Jacob recognizes that a comprehensive description of the African-American circumstance must include attention to other aspects of disadvantaged social existence. Jacob says, "the gap between blacks and whites extends beyond poverty and unemployment rates to include all the key indices of life" (SBA/89 p. 4). Accordingly, the Urban League's 1989 report contains reflection upon other aspects of the African-American circumstance. In addition to Jacob, there are ten other contributors — including Charles V. Hamilton.

These essays represent a variety of socio-scientific and cultural areas. Each contributor was asked to describe the disadvantage of African-Americans in a given area of social existence, and to offer public policy recommendations for improving upon this circumstance. Jacob says, "we have asked contributors to this volume of our annual State of Black America report to focus on parity within their given areas — how wide the gap is, what is needed to close it, and what public policy initiatives will be necessary to close the gap" (SBA/89 p. 6).

The essay focusing on parity in the area of economics by David Swinton is more descriptive than prescriptive. It serves to reinforce and elaborate upon the perception of a growing socio-economic inequality between blacks and whites in the United States. Swinton's purpose is to provide the Bush administration with "a clear understanding of the large magnitude of the problem of economic disparities as a precondition of finding effective remedies to the problem" (SBA/89 p. 9). Swinton measures the economic gap by reference to per capita income, family income, aggregate income, ownership of property and businesses, employment, occupational status, and earning rates. Based upon an analysis of data from the U.S. Department of Commerce, Bureau of the Census, Money, Income and Poverty Status in 1987, previous Urban League reports, and other sources, Swinton concludes:

> First, racial inequality in economic life is still the norm throughout America. Second, the magnitude of the parity gaps is very large in all

dimensions. Third, the disparities have been worsening in most dimensions for at least the past ten years. If present trends continue, we can have no expectation or hope of attaining economic parity in economic life in the foreseeable future. [SBA/89 pp. 35–36]

With regard to what must be done to reverse these trends, Swinton maintains that "the most important ingredient of all for bringing about racial parity is a commitment at the highest levels of the administration to make this a high priority" (SBA/89 p. 39). He says it is "the responsibility of the Bush administration" to lead a comprehensive national effort, which includes "a substantial capital development component," to achieve racial parity in economic life (SBA/89 pp. 38–39).

In the area of political life, contributor Charles V. Hamilton measures the gap between black and white political empowerment by reference to three criteria: (1) political participation, (2) public attitudes, and (3) public policies.

When political participation is measured by voter turnout, Hamilton says, "blacks are reaching parity in a shrinking area of activity" (SBA/89 p. 114). That is to say, while African-Americans are starting to vote in percentages that approximate those of white voters, nonetheless the total percentage of citizens who vote is declining. When political participation is measured by the number of black elected officials, Hamilton finds that while the last two decades have witnessed a dramatic increase in the number of black elected officials, still blacks have not reached political parity. Prescriptively, Hamilton says, "The goal in voting should not be, it seems, to aim for 'parity,' but to seek the goal of maximum registration and turnout" (SBA/89 p. 114).

In regard to public attitudes, Hamilton says, "in a real sense we cannot expect significant political empowerment of blacks if the attitudes of whites and blacks on a range of important issues are not shared" (SBA/89 p. 115). He allows that "one should not reject the possibility, slight or great, of changing unfavorable attitudes" (SBA/89 p. 118). Also, in regard to the role of the Supreme Court, Hamilton believes that the court's current tendency need not doom black political empowerment if blacks use the vote to pressure the legislative and executive branches to take up the slack.

While political participation and changing attitudes are important indicators of political empowerment, ultimately, says Hamilton, the best way to measure black political empowerment is to focus on public policy agenda. Then we can measure black political empowerment by simply comparing what we asked for with what we got. Hamilton prescribes that the various organizations and groups that represent the black constituency "come together and fashion a reasonably coherent, unified policy agenda," which takes the form of "quite specific actionable proposals" (SBA/89 p. 120).

In the area of sociology, contributor Robert B. Hill finds that black families in the U.S.A. are suffering a debilitating instability that is a direct function of increasing economic instability:

> While black unemployment soared from six percent to 20 percent between 1969 and 1983 due to four back-to-back recessions, the proportion of female-headed black families jumped from 28 percent to 42 percent. Each percentage point rise in black unemployment was correlated with a comparable increase in one-parent black families. [SBA/89 p. 41]

Hill goes on to say that black families in the U.S.A. are suffering disadvantage in other areas such as crime, gang violence, drug trafficking, drug-related homicides, life expectancy, homelessness, and inadequate housing. Given the continuation of these trends, Hill summarizes his predictions for the future of black families:

> In sum, between 1988 and 2000: (a) the median age of the black population will rise from 27.1 to 30.2 years; (b) the total black population will increase from 30.5 to 35.7 million; (c) the number of female-headed black families (+25 percent) will increase twice as fast as the number of black married couples (+11 percent); and (d) the proportion of black families headed by women will rise from 44 to 48 percent. [SBA/89 p. 46]

And Hill projects that by 2000 the black unemployment rate will be more than double that of whites (SBA/89 p. 49). "If concerted efforts are not taken to reduce the alarming rates of high school dropouts, functional illiteracy, and declines in college and graduate school enrollments among minorities, this nation will be sharply polarized by the year 2000 between high-paying jobs held largely by whites and low-paying jobs held largely by blacks and Hispanics" (SBA/89 p. 50).

In order to prevent these dire projections from becoming reality, and in order to achieve black/white parity by the year 2000, Hill prescribes that the public and private sectors must "successfully confront several important issues: attaining economic self-sufficiency; strengthening and stabilizing families; and developing viable and healthy communities" (SBA/89 p. 49).

In order to contribute to economic self-sufficiency, Hill prescribes that the poor and jobless not "bear the brunt of deficit-reduction policies during the 1990s" (SBA/89 p. 51); that government enact tax reforms "to enhance economic self-sufficiency among poor and working-class families" (SBA/89 p. 51); and that government enact welfare reforms that include increased in-kind benefits that more effectively target the poor (SBA/89 pp. 51–52).

In order to contribute to stronger and more stable black families, Hill prescribes "comprehensive strategies ... to combat adolescent pregnancy in black families during the 1990s" (SBA/89 p. 53); "more sensitive child support policies . . . to enhance the functioning of single-parent black families" (SBA/89 p. 53); increased day-care facilities (SBA/89 p. 54); "more sensitive foster care policies . . . that build on the informal adoption and foster care practices among blacks" (SBA/89 p. 55); increased attention by government and the black community to drug abuse, AIDS, and alcohol abuse (SBA/89 p. 55–56); and increased attention ("highest priority") "to insuring that black boys, male youth, adult men, and fathers are able to fulfill their responsibilities as productive members of this society" (SBA/89 p. 56).

In order to develop more viable and healthy black communities, Hill prescribes comprehensive public and private sector efforts to remedy residential segregation via "bold housing initiatives" (SBA/89 p. 57), community development programs (SBA/89 pp. 57–58), and economic development programs (SBA/89 p. 58).

In addition to offering general social ethical prescriptions for bringing black families into parity with whites by the year 2000, Hill also offers strategies for implementing these prescriptions. The "key guiding principles" behind Hill's strategizing include a recognition that what is needed are partnership and coalition efforts between all segments of society—the public sector, the private sector, and the black community, including its community-based organizations and churches; a commitment to combat racism; attention to family impact analyses; and attention to cost-effective targeting (SBA/89 p. 59).

Strategically, Hill says his prescriptions for achieving economic self-sufficiency must proceed from a public policy commitment not "to fight inflation by inducing recessions" (SBA/89 p. 59), and from a rededication to "the goals of the Employment Act of 1946 and the Humphrey-Hawkins Act of 1978 to provide everyone willing and able to work with jobs at liveable wages" (SBA/89 p. 59). Also, public policy strategy must include enhanced job-training programs and a reformed AFDC program with a higher income ceiling for eligibility (SBA/89 p. 60). The prescriptions for strengthening black families must include focused aid to single-parent families in the form of remedial education, classroom and work experience, affordable day care and medical care, decent housing, child support enforcement, family violence assistance, enhanced parenting skills, counseling, mentoring, special aid for young fathers, expanded child care, a children's allowance, and reformed foster care (SBA/89 pp. 60–61). The prescriptions for developing more viable communities are said to require public policy strategies that include increased supplies of low-income housing, increased home-ownership options for low-income families, and economic development efforts that target inner city and public housing sites (SBA/89 p. 61).

Additionally, Hill applauds the efforts of black churches to work in these areas, and he recommends partnership and coalition efforts that employ churches and other community-based organizations as "major conduits, contractors, sub-contractors, advisors, etc." (SBA/89 p. 59). Finally, he concludes that "black churches should be encouraged to expand into economic development efforts" (SBA/89 p. 61).

Marian Wright Edelman, president of the Children's Defense Fund, contributes to the Urban League's 1989 report an essay focusing on the status of black children in the U.S.A. – "Black Children in America." Edelman reports that "black children, youth, and families remain worse off than whites on every economic indicator of American life – and the gap is widening" (SBA/89 p. 65). She measures this gap by pointing out that, in 1987, 45 percent of black children lived in poverty as compared with only 15 percent of white children (SBA/89 p. 65). And she laments that programs designed to help lift children out of poverty have been cut drastically during the 1980s.

Edelman predicts that as the U.S.A. moves into the twenty-first century, "unless we change this country's course, many black children will be left behind completely, suffering from poor health care and nutrition, stifled by inadequate education and training, and trapped in lives of impoverishment and despair" (SBA/89 p. 63). She goes on to argue that the future prosperity of the nation is jeopardized by this circumstance (SBA/89 p. 64).

Edelman prescribes that "what America needs is a comprehensive, long-term investment in policies and programs which help all poor children and their families" (SBA/89 p. 64). She argues that such programs should include provisions for affordable and quality child care, and that the federal government should play a significant role in providing such child care for low-income working parents (SBA/89 p. 69). Also, Edelman prescribes increased federal support for health and nutrition programs, and increased attention to quality early education, and to improved basic skills for black students (SBA/89 pp. 71–73). Moreover, she argues that because the well-being of black children is dependent upon the socio-economic well-being of black families generally, in order to help the children, it is necessary to help their families out of poverty (SBA/89 p.72).

Edelman's public policy recommendations include support for the congressional bill, Act for Better Child Care Services; funding for WIC programs, increased Medicaid coverage and immunization programs for all children; increased funding for Head Start and Chapter 1 programs; and a minimum wage of $4.65 by 1990 (SBA/89 pp. 75–76).

With respect to education, housing, health, substance abuse, and other indicators of social well-being, the other Urban League studies offer similar descriptions of the African-American circumstance. Across the board, the gap between black and white U.S. citizens has been increasing for the past two decades. If we allow these trends to continue, we can expect coming generations of African-Americans to be increasingly and disproportionately represented among the truly disadvantaged.[6]

Rather than allow such a dismal future, the Urban League, along with other liberal sociology, prescribes that it should be a matter of national policy to engage in massive and comprehensive coalition efforts – including the private sector and the black community—to reverse the trends toward increasing social disadvantage. Here again, the obvious social ethical implication for black churches is that, insofar as they are concerned to contribute to the reversal of increasing socio-economic disadvantage, they should participate in such coalition efforts. Robert Hill, for example, says explicitly, "black churches should be encouraged to expand into economic development efforts" (SBA/89 p. 61). Black churches, and other neighborhood-based organizations and groups, he adds, should serve as major conduits between government resources and disadvantaged people.

C. Eric Lincoln's contribution to the Urban League's 1989 report is a helpful reflection upon the identity and role of the black church in the continuing struggle to overcome the heritage of slavery and subsequent oppression and dislocation. Lincoln says the black church was "the nurturing mother of black freedom" (SBA/89 p. 146). He calls the independent black church movement "the first black stride toward freedom and responsibility" (SBA/89 p. 137). The genius of the black church, says Lincoln, is that it recognizes that we have both spiritual and material needs, and moreover, the good news is that the black church "is moving to address these needs, not with perfect symmetry, but with persistence" (SBA/89 p. 147).

While Lincoln's essay is all but exclusively descriptive, he does express approval of "the fact that black churches are not only cooperating with each other, they are increasingly willing to work closely with secular institutions in the struggle against the mundane challenges to the physical well-being of the black community" (SBA/89 p. 149). This clearly suggests that Lincoln believes our churches should continue to engage in liberal coalition efforts to improve the circumstances of disadvantaged populations.

The characteristic liberal conviction that public and other sectors of society should develop comprehensive and affirmative (not merely trickle-down) policies aimed at improving the status of disadvantaged populations is a secular or theologically unreflective version of our social ethic of breaking bread. The social ethical reflections of secular (theologically unreflective) liberal social science affirm that we ought to contribute to the comprehensive socio-economic-political empowerment of the people. In regard to this general affirmation, liberal social ethics is in agreement with the ethic of breaking bread—a social ethic that I regard as appropriate to every social location. Accordingly, black theological social ethical reflection supports the bread-breaking aspects of liberal coalition agenda.

While we now find that black theological social ethics supports the general idea of coalition efforts to remedy socio-economic disadvantage through bread-breaking public policies, there remain particular aspects of liberal social ethical prescriptions that require a more detailed consideration—especially in regard to the precise role of our churches. In the next chapter I shall examine more specific features of liberal coalition agenda from the churchly perspective of black theology.

NOTES

1. J. Deotis Roberts, in his article "The Holy Spirit and Liberation: A Black Perspective" in the *A. M. E. Zion Quarterly Review* (January 1985), says "The black church is operating in the power of the Spirit which moves from worship to social involvement, as it has frequently done throughout its history" (p. 28). Similarly, James H. Cone, in his essay "Sanctification and Liberation in the Black Religious Tradition with Special Reference to Black Worship" in his book *Speaking the Truth: Ecumenism, Liberation, and Black Theology* (Grand Rapids: William B. Eerdmans, 1986), describes the presence of the Holy Spirit in African-American worship as a "liberating experience" that confirms God's presence in the struggle for freedom and empowers worshipers to engage the struggle with renewed courage (pp. 18–19).

2. J. Deotis Roberts calls black theology to increased cross-cultural dialogical activity in his book *Black Theology in Dialogue* (Philadelphia: Westminster Press, 1987). James H. Cone, in *Speaking the Truth: Ecumenism, Liberation, and Black Theology* (Grand Rapids: William B. Eerdmans, 1986), joins Third World theologians in insisting upon "a definition of ecumenism that moved beyond the traditional interconfessional issues to the problems of poverty and the struggle for social and economic justice in a global context" (p. 142). In *For My People* (Maryknoll, N.Y.: Orbis Books, 1984) Cone offers a critical assessment of black theology's origin and development, which prescribes that in the future black theology should engage in increased dialogue with other ethnic groups and with Third World peoples from around the world so as to yield an enlarged vision of liberation that attends to global circumstances and to the various interconnected forms of oppression.

3. In *Black Power: The Politics of Liberation in America* (New York: Vintage Books, 1967) Stokely Carmichael and Charles V. Hamilton identify four preconditions for viable coalition efforts. They are: "(a) the recognition by the parties involved of their respective self-interests; (b) the mutual belief that each party stands to benefit in terms of that self-interest from allying with the other or others; (c) the acceptance of the fact that each party has its own independent base of power and does not depend for ultimate decision-making on a force outside itself; and (d) the realization that the coalition deals with specific and identifiable—as opposed to general and vague—goals" (pp. 79–80).

4. For historical examples of black churchly involvement in liberal coalition efforts during the civil rights movement in Chicago, see Alan B. Anderson and George W. Pickering, *Confronting the Color Line: The Broken Promise of the Civil Rights Movement in Chicago* (Athens: University of Georgia Press, 1986).

5. Daniel Patrick Moynihan, *The Negro Family: The Case for National Action* (Washington, D.C.: Office of Policy Planning and Research, U.S. Department of Labor, 1965).

6. Similar socio-scientific descriptions and predictions are offered by the Committee on the Status of Black Americans in their 1989 report—*A Common Destiny: Blacks and American Society* (Washington, D.C.: National Academy Press, 1989). This twenty-two member committee includes Charles V. Hamilton and William Julius Wilson. In the preface to this 608-page report, Gerald David Jaynes (study director) and Robin M. Williams, Jr. (chair), report "striking resemblances"

between the committee's description of the status of black Americans in 1989 and the 1968 Kerner report (*Report of the National Advisory Commission on Civil Disorders*, Otto Kerner, chair), which concluded that the U.S.A. is moving toward two racially separate and unequal societies (pp. x-xi). Like the Urban League's 1989 report, the Committee on the Status of Black Americans reports increasing relative socio-economic disadvantage during the previous two decades (pp. 6-7). Similarly, the committee foresees, in the absence of major public policy initiatives, an increasingly difficult future for underclass black U.S. populations (p. 26). Also see Jeremiah Cotton, "The Declining Relative Economic Status of Black Families," *The Review of Black Political Economy*, vol. 18, no. 1 (Summer 1989).

BIBLIOGRAPHY

Anderson, Alan B., and George W. Pickering. *Confronting the Color Line: The Broken Promise of the Civil Rights Movement in Chicago*. Athens: University of Georgia Press, 1986.

Calmore, John O. "To Make Wrong Right: The Necessary and Proper Aspirations of Fair Housing." *The State of Black America 1989*. New York: National Urban League, 1989.

Carmichael, Stokely, and Charles V. Hamilton. *Black Power: The Politics of Liberation in America*. New York: Vintage Books, 1967.

Cobbs, Price M. "Valuing Diversity: The Myth and the Challenge." *The State of Black America 1989*. New York: National Urban League, 1989.

Cone, James H. *For My People*. Maryknoll, N.Y.: Orbis Books, 1984.

———. *Speaking the Truth: Ecumenism, Liberation, and Black Theology*. Grand Rapids: William B. Eerdmans, 1986.

Cotton, Jeremiah. "The Declining Relative Economic Status of Black Families." *The Review of Black Political Economy*, vol. 18, no. 1 (Summer 1989).

Dewart, Janet, ed. *The State of Black America 1989*. New York: National Urban League, Inc., 1989.

Edelman, Marian Wright. "Black Children in America." *The State of Black America 1989*. New York: National Urban League, 1989.

Gamwell, Franklin I. *Beyond Preference: Liberal Theories of Independent Associations*. Chicago: University of Chicago Press, 1984.

Hamilton, Charles V. "On Parity and Political Empowerment." *The State of Black America 1989*. New York: National Urban League, 1989.

Hill, Robert B. "Critical Issues for Black Families by the Year 2000." *The State of Black America 1989*. New York: National Urban League, 1989.

Jacob, John E. "Black America, 1988: An Overview." *The State of Black America 1989*. New York: National Urban League, 1989.

Jaynes, Gerald David, and Robin M. Williams, Jr., eds. *A Common Destiny: Blacks and American Society*, prepared by the Committee on the Status of Black Americans, the Commission on Behavioral and Social Sciences and Education, and the National Research Council. Washington, D.C.: National Academy Press, 1989.

Lincoln, C. Eric. "Knowing the Black Church: What It Is and Why." *The State of Black America 1989*. New York: National Urban League, 1989.

Moynihan, Daniel Patrick. *The Negro Family: The Case for National Action*. Washington, D. C.: Office of Policy Planning and Research, U.S. Department of Labor, 1965.

Nobles, Wade W., and Lawford L. Goddard. "Drugs in the African-American Community: Clear and Present Danger." *The State of Black America 1989*. New York: National Urban League, 1989.

Roberts, J. Deotis. *Black Theology in Dialogue*. Philadelphia: Westminster Press, 1987.

———. "The Holy Spirit and Liberation: A Black Perspective." *A.M.E. Zion Quarterly Review* (January 1985).

Swinton, David H. "Economic Status of Black Americans." *The State of Black America 1989*. New York: National Urban League, 1989.

Wilson, Reginald. "Black Higher Education: Crisis and Promise." *The State of Black America 1989*. New York: National Urban League, 1989.

Wilson, William Julius. *The Declining Significance of Race*. Chicago: University of Chicago Press, 1978.

———. *The Truly Disadvantaged: The Inner City, the Underclass, and Public Policy*. Chicago: University of Chicago Press, 1987.

CHAPTER FOUR

The Fruitful Multiplication of Righteousness

Analyzing Liberal Coalition Agenda from the Churchly Perspective of Black Theology

We have already seen that the philosophy of black power and the elder tradition of the independent black church movement authorize black theology's interest in the possibility of coalition efforts. And from the perspective of liberal sociology, it has been suggested that our churches should participate in liberal coalition efforts. *It is now time to assess the social ethical views offered by liberal sociology in the 1980s from the churchly perspective of black theological social ethics.*

Our Christian social ethical conviction is that the ethic of breaking bread is appropriate to every social location. The characteristic liberal conviction that public and other sectors of society ought to contribute to the well-being and empowerment of all, including especially disadvantaged populations, is a theologically unreflective or secular version of the ethic of breaking bread. Accordingly, black theology affirms this bread-breaking aspect of liberal social ethical reflection, but we are careful to evaluate liberal social ethical prescriptions and policies with an eye to the difference between bread and crumbs. We shall employ the unity of social ethical convictions represented by the King-McKissick-Carmichael coalition of 1966 as a way of measuring the distance between the breaking of bread and distribution of crumbs.

LIBERAL COALITION EFFORTS ACCORDING TO KING, McKISSICK, AND CARMICHAEL-HAMILTON

King's social ethical prescriptions suggest that a righteous liberal coalition effort should include such changes in the U.S. socio-economic-labor-market structures as will serve to abolish poverty:

I am convinced that the simplest approach will prove to be the most effective—the solution to poverty is to abolish it directly by a now widely discussed measure: the guaranteed income. [WDWGFH p. 162]

The problem indicates that our emphasis must be two fold. We must create full employment or we must create incomes. ... New forms of work that enhance the social good will have to be devised for those for whom traditional jobs are not available. [WDWGFH p. 163]

Furthermore, King pegs the reference point for abolition of poverty in the U.S.A. to the median U.S. income:

Two conditions are indispensable if we are to ensure that the guaranteed income operates as a consistently progressive measure. First, it must be pegged to the median income of society, not at the lowest levels of income. ... Second, the guaranteed income must be dynamic; it must automatically increase as the total social income grows. [WDWGFH p. 164]

And, as is consistent with Wilson's public relations advice, and with the philosophy of black power, King points out that such programs "would benefit all the poor, including the two-thirds of those who are white" (WDWGFH p. 165).

King is consistent with the philosophy of black power also in holding that, in our bread-breaking effort to abolish poverty, we must not fail to include the poor outside the United States. King insists we must contribute to solving the problem of poverty on an international scale (WDWGFH pp. 176–77). King says that "the wealthy nations of the world must promptly initiate a massive, sustained Marshall Plan for Asia, Africa and South America" (WDWGFH p. 178). And again, emphasizing the benefits that would pertain to all people, King says "a genuine program on the part of the wealthy nations to make prosperity a reality for the poor nations will in the final analysis enlarge the prosperity of all" (WDWGFH p. 180).

McKissick's analysis suggests that a truly liberating coalition agenda must include massive and "equitable redistribution of land, wealth, and power" (TFM p. 156). McKissick prescribes a national public policy agenda (an agenda consistent with the U.S. Constitution and Declaration of Independence and with a philosophy of black nationalism) that seeks to sequester land within U.S. borders for the development of a separate black nation (TFM p. 155). McKissick's coalition agenda includes:

Ownership of the land area in places such as Harlem and Bedford Stuyvesant must be transferred to the residents, individually or collectively. [TFM p. 156]

Ownership of businesses in the ghetto must be transferred to Black People, either individually or collectively. [TFM p. 156]

All government facilities in the ghetto must be run and operated by Black People. [TFM p. 156]

In all ghetto areas of the United States, Black universities must be established. These universities should be staffed and run by Blacks, with curricula concentrating on Black history, Black culture, and a collection of historical information pertinent to Black People. [TFM p. 157]

McKissick's proposal for liberating coalition efforts also includes an insistence upon changes in the U.S. economic base such that we will cease profiting from and being dependent upon the exploitation and subjugation of Third World economies (TFM p. 151). McKissick, then, proposes coalition efforts that include the equitable sharing of land, resources, economic, political, and other power with African-Americans and other disadvantaged and oppressed peoples throughout the world.

Ultimately, Carmichael and Hamilton would like to see blacks and others engage in genuinely liberating coalition efforts (BP p. 84). But at that stage of our struggle—1967—they prescribed that we must first, "close ranks," "reorient," define ourselves as black and as African-American, and redefine our relations to others (BP pp. 34–39). Then—"the next step"—we must begin the process of "political modernization." Political modernization includes:

(1) questioning old values and institutions of the society; (2) searching for new and different forms of political structure to solve political and economic problems; and (3) broadening the base of political participation to include more people in the decision-making process. [BP p. 39]

Through the process of political modernization, we could develop an independent base of power with which to bargain and with which to contribute to some future coalition effort.

In 1967 Carmichael and Hamilton argued that, on account of the absence of an independent base of political power controlled by the decisions of black people, political coalition efforts were unrealistic and premature (BP pp. 80–84, 96). They said, "there is a clear need for genuine power bases before black people can enter into coalitions" (BP p. 78). Accordingly, *Black Power: The Politics of Liberation in America* is not much concerned with what items should be on a liberal coalition agenda; but it is clear that they would like to see a major redistribution of wealth and power (BP pp. 47, 66):

Our basic premise is that money and jobs are not the final answer to the black man's problems . . . the basic goal is not "welfare colonialism," as some have called the anti-poverty and other federal programs, but the inclusion of black people at all levels of decision-making. We do not seek to be mere recipients from the decision-making process but participants in it. [BP p. 183]

Therefore, a coalition agenda consistent with Carmichael and Hamilton's philosophy of black power would have to include provisions for vastly more inclusive input at all levels of decision-making.

In some ways Carmichael and Hamilton's 1967 text remains an appropriate description of our political circumstance as we begin the 1990s. For the most part, we African-Americans in the U.S.A. still have no national, and few local, independent bases of political power. By this measure, in our political life we have not yet achieved the kinds of relatively independent black controlled institutions, structures, and political parties prerequisite to the possibility of our engaging in genuinely liberating coalition politics. However, as we have already seen, in our religious associations — unlike our political and other associations — we have achieved, by way of the black church revolution, the kind of relative independence and power of self-determination necessary to admit the possibility of our engaging in genuinely liberating coalition efforts. Therefore it is appropriate that our churches, and other racially separate and independently empowered black associations, consider whether specific features of prescribed liberal coalition agenda are consistent with our ethic of breaking bread.

On the one hand, liberal social thought is consistent with an ethic of breaking bread insofar as it maintains that public and other sectors of society should make affirmative contributions to the well-being of all. But on the other hand, liberal social policies have been and continue to be about distributing crumbs, not about breaking bread. According to the measure indicated by the liberating social ethical prescriptions of King, McKissick, and Carmichael and Hamilton, most federal, state, philanthropic, and volunteer social welfare efforts in the U.S.A. are about distributing crumbs rather than breaking bread. Genuine bread breaking entails wholesale and more equitable distribution of wealth, resources, land, opportunity, and power. Liberal social policies almost never approximate such genuinely bread-breaking ideals. The kinds of massive changes in socio-economic-labor-market structures advocated by William Julius Wilson in his effort to improve the life-chances of all disadvantaged U.S. citizens, and the massive public and private efforts prescribed by the National Urban League to achieve black-white economic parity in the U.S.A., come somewhat closer to bread breaking than present and past liberal social welfare policies.

Ultimately, from the churchly perspective of black theological social ethics, while the bread-breaking aspects of liberal thought are to be affirmed, our churchly conviction is that secular liberal philosophies are philosophically inadequate insofar as they are uninformed by theological and religious reflection.[1] Liberal public policy efforts in the U.S.A. have been and continue to be morally and functionally inadequate because they are by our measure virtually always about the distribution and management of crumbs rather than the actual sharing of bread. Moreover, because liberal public policies fail so consistently to approximate the bread-breaking aspects of liberal ideals, in many communities, especially in Third World communities, the term "liberal" has come to designate the support of crumb distribution programs, while the advocacy of genuine bread-breaking public policy is spoken of as "radical." When the terms liberal and radical take on these meanings, black theological social ethical reflection is better described as radical.

EXCLUSIVE CONCERN FOR U.S. CITIZENS AS A PROBLEM

We have already acknowledged that black theology is more inclusive than African-American theology, and I also acknowledge that African-American theology is more inclusive than the theology of African-Americans in the United States. Therefore, from the more inclusive perspective of black theological social ethics, we regret the fact that so much of the liberal sociology and social ethics in the U.S.A. is concerned almost exclusively with the well-being of U.S. citizens. Parity 2000, for example, seeks to bring black U.S. citizens into parity with white citizens, and it sometimes appears to pursue the interest of black citizens to the neglect of or at the expense of noncitizens—legal and, in particular, illegal immigrants. For example, Robert Hill in his contribution to *The State of Black America 1989* lists "increased competition from Hispanic and Asian immigrants" as a "critical issue confronting black families" (p. 50). Without further qualification, this could be understood to imply that we should not allow the present immigration rate to continue, because it contributes to the disadvantage of black U.S. citizens.

While we certainly are U.S. citizens, our self-understanding and our range of concerns is not exclusively described by U.S. citizenship. From a cross-generational perspective, before we were Americans, we were Africans. On this side of the Atlantic, long before most of us were acknowledged as fully human U.S. citizens, black churches were regularly referring to our people as Abyssinian, Ethiopian, and African. A vision of our church history that extends across only a few generations will indicate that we are African and American, in that order.[2]

This double consciousness, which W. E. B. DuBois attributes to the very "souls of black folk," implies double allegiance. Our allegiance to red-black-green-gold is no less significant than our allegiance to red-white-blue. To be sure, there have been many times in the black experience when red-white-blue was waved by our oppressors. Black and red—especially red—

and brown Americans have often experienced exclusion, oppression, chattel enslavement, and genocide under the banner of red-white-blue. For many Third World and colored peoples, Old Glory has regularly failed to serve as a liberation flag. Red-black-green-gold represents a more inclusive allegiance, an allegiance that includes black and African people all over the world. As a symbol of liberation, it represents allegiance with those who best contribute land, wealth, and blood to the struggle for freedom and empowerment.

The philosophy of black power and the elder tradition of our independent black churches provide us with a range of concern that does not exclude or neglect the well-being of people who are not U.S. citizens. While Carmichael and Hamilton's text on black power is primarily about the exercise of black political power within the U.S.A., as our text is primarily about the exercise of black church power within the U.S.A., nonetheless, they understand that the struggle for freedom and empowerment has a more inclusive context. For example, they say:

> If we succeed, we will exercise control over our lives, politically, economically and psychically. We will also contribute to the development of a viable larger society; in terms of ultimate social benefit, there is nothing unilateral about the movement to free black people. [BP p. vii]

The same point is made by another major figure in the black liberation struggle—the late Huey P. Newton—who as the Black Panther Party's "Servant of the People" declared,

> Our goal is to destroy all elements of oppression. We pledge ourselves to end imperialism and distribute the wealth of the world to all the people of the world. [Huey P. Newton, *To Die For the People: The Writings of Huey P. Newton*, p. 42]

Also, our religious leader in the struggle, Martin Luther King, Jr., taught us that "a threat to justice anywhere in the world is a threat to justice everywhere in the world." Moreover, King said that he could not segregate his concern for the liberation of Negroes in the U.S.A. from his concern for the liberation of Southeast Asia from U.S. military activity. Carmichael, Hamilton, McKissick, Newton, Malcolm, and King are clear that our struggle is not exclusively about the liberation of black people in the U.S.A., but about freedom and justice for all people everywhere.

Black power and black religion require that our commitment to the struggle for freedom and empowerment be not circumscribed by U.S. borders, by U.S. citizenship, or by the national interest. "Let freedom ring" and "power to the people" do not mean freedom and power only to black people in the U.S.A. Freedom and power to the people means freedom and power to all the people.

To the extent that our liberal socio-scientific resources are concerned with the well-being of U.S. citizens to the neglect of others, we must lament and repent of such negligence. Many of the truly disadvantaged within our country, along our borders, and elsewhere, are not U.S. citizens—though they may still be Americans. Insofar as our existence affects them, any social ethical reflection that neglects concern with their well-being is, at best, morally problematic. Moreover, any social ethical prescription that deliberately seeks to exclude these neglected ones from the breaking of bread is, from our point of view, morally reprehensible.

Robert Hill and other social scientists may be correct in finding that the current influx of legal and illegal immigrants is contributing to a slack labor market, and that a slack labor market contributes to the disadvantage of African-Americans.[3] But our churches, on account of our Christian commitment to the ethic of breaking bread, are not able to endorse strictly exclusionary tactics as the solution to this problem. From our point of view, it may be that the way to keep the rising number of refugees and immigrants from contributing to our socio-economic disadvantage is not by walling them out, but by contributing to improved conditions in the places they are leaving. Too often it is the case that they are seeking refuge here because our nation has helped to make their original homes uninhabitable. Rather than joining a national coalition to build more impenetrable walls and borders, or being co-opted by crumb-distribution programs, we would rather share such bread and other resources as will enable our neighbors to stay where they might rather be in the first place. We are committed to the empowerment of all the people through the ethic of breaking bread, not to the empowerment of some through the exclusion of others.

LIBERAL VIEWS ON STRENGTHENING BLACK FAMILIES

Throughout Wilson's *Truly Disadvantaged*, and throughout the Urban League's 1989 report, and in numerous other social scientific studies from the 1980s, the circumstance of African-American families in the U.S.A. is described with alarm. As is consistent with Wilson's findings regarding the unfavorable African-American male marriageable pool index,[4] Hill, Edelman (SBA/89 pp. 67–68), and others report an increasing scarcity of marriageable black males. Robert Hill attributes the increasing scarcity of marriageable black men to a "gauntlet of school expulsions, special education placements, dropouts, foster care placements, delinquency, arrests, incarceration, unemployment, drug addiction, alcohol abuse, homelessness, homicides, and suicides from the cradle to the grave" (SBA/89 p. 56). Moreover, to make bad conditions worse, it is widely reported that young blacks in the U.S.A. are increasingly less likely to marry, more likely to separate and divorce, and less likely to remarry than other U.S. citizens.[5]

Broken homes, "female-headed" or more precisely, adult male-absent families,[6] out of wedlock and teenage pregnancies, welfare dependency, and poverty are increasing at alarming rates. The well-being of most black children is increasingly at risk. Today one-half of black children in the U.S.A. live in poverty.[7] And other difficulties associated with poverty, such as drug abuse, disease, and crime, are surging upward. William Julius Wilson, the contributors to the Urban League's 1989 report, and many other contemporary social analysts report that many, if not most, though certainly not all, African-American families are suffering serious economic and social difficulties.

We know of course that sociology has been concerned about the social conditions faced by African-American families since the time and work of W. E. B. DuBois, and more recently since Daniel P. Moynihan's famous study.[8] However, the difference between what sociologists were saying before the 1970s and what was being said in the 1980s suggests that in a short period of time things have gone from bad to very bad to much worse. And as bad as this is, we may expect even greater deprivation, suffering, and "social dislocation" in the future. Social scientists regularly predict that, in the absence of massive and comprehensive socio-economic policies working to the contrary, our circumstance in the 1990s and beyond will be even worse, probably much worse, than what we now endure. Social scientists are now describing the current and future circumstance of African-American families in the U.S.A. in such dire terms as "crisis," "endangered," "in peril," "at risk," "catastrophic," and even "coming extinction" and "genocide."[9] According to what many social scientists are presently saying, it appears that the social and economic viability of African-American families in the U.S.A. is now at greater risk than at any time since slavery and the great transatlantic impress.

In contrast to the primary emphasis of the Urban League upon economic parity by the year 2000 and Wilson's primary prescriptions for changes in economic and social organization, much of the social and public policy analysis in recent years has focused upon African-American birth rates. Frequently, we are told that the problem with black families is that we are having too many babies—especially illegitimate babies, and that the solution to the problem is to find ways to reduce this birth rate—especially among black teenagers. This is the now infamous "problem" of "black teenage pregnancy."

Actually, Wilson, Hill, Edelman, and others have shown that the so-called explosion in black teenage pregnancies is a myth. Nonetheless, the pregnancy rate among unmarried black teenagers is high,[10] and liberal sociology is virtually unanimous in its concern, in Hill's words, to "combat adolescent pregnancy in black families" (SBA/89 p. 53). Hill and others believe that strengthening and stabilizing black families must include "comprehensive strategies" to "combat adolescent pregnancy in black families during the 1990s" (SBA/89 p. 53). Such strategies typically include: providing "sex education," which includes information about prescribed sexual abstinence, safe sex, contraception, and birth control; increased availability of condoms and other contraceptive instruments, treatments, and techniques; and various pregnancy prevention, pregnancy termination, birth control, and "family planning" programs.

The advocates of black power tend to reject the idea that stabilizing and strengthening African-American families is accomplished simply, if at all, by cutting the birth rate in African-American communities. To be sure, many black power advocates regard established "family planning" programs as instruments of genocide insofar as they tend to be concerned almost exclusively with contraceptive techniques.

Rather than preventing the birth of our children into conditions of poverty and dislocation by preventing the birth of these beautiful ones, we propose to prevent the birth of children into conditions of poverty and dislocation by preventing poverty and dislocation. The solution to the problem of children born to welfare-dependent families is not preventing the birth of the children, but freeing the families from unemployment and welfare dependency. The solution to the problem of unwed motherhood is not increased contraception, but increased numbers of weddings. The problem of disadvantaged and socially dislocated children is not addressed primarily, if at all, by family planning programs concerned mainly with preventing their conception or birth. From a cross-generational perspective, this is genocide against the beautiful ones who are not yet born. The problem of disadvantaged and socially dislocated children is best addressed by programs offering advantage and wholesome social location. We need policies of opportunity and empowerment so that we may fruitfully multiply rather than simply multiply, and we need programs designed to prevent us from multiplying at all, not at all.

Scripture calls us to "be fruitful and multiply." We are already good at multiplication. Now we need to add fruitfulness rather than simply subtracting multiplication. From the perspective of black power, and from the perspective of our appropriation of Scripture, we need comprehensive social empowerment for fruitful procreativity; that is, we need genuine family planning rather than contraceptives, postponed marriages, and planning not to be family. We need continued multiplication plus empowerment, rather than continued disadvantage minus multiplication.

While it is permitted for secular institutions to "combat adolescent pregnancy" by prescribing condoms and other contraceptive devices and techniques, African-American churches are not willing to do the same. Insofar as we hold to the traditional church view that sex outside marriage is illegitimate, our churches are not able to prescribe contraceptive and safe-sex techniques to unmarried persons — adolescent or adult. Moreover, it has never been our tradition to prescribe against adolescent or young-adult sex and procreativity per se; instead, it has been our tradition to oppose sex outside marriage whether adolescent or adult. By our measure, the only "safe sex" is sex within the committed bounds of marriage and family.

Inasmuch as African-American churches seek to combat sexual activity outside marriage rather than adolescent and young-adult pregnancy per se, for us, "family planning" should be more about marriage counseling and planning to be family than about extramarital methods of contraception. Instead of condoms and sexual technique, we prescribe premarital abstinence followed by sexual procreativity within marriage. According to traditional African-American wisdom and church ethics, family planning ought to be guided by the view that the beginning of sexual activity and the beginning of married life should not be much removed from each other.

There is, of course, a secular realism that compels us to grant that we are not likely to be at all successful in prescribing prolonged sexual abstinence in a society that is so thoroughly preoccupied with sexuality in entertainment, fashion, marketing, and elsewhere. What is even more discouraging is the fact that virtually all adolescent African-Americans in the U.S.A. experience the onset of sexual urges and procreative capacities long before they achieve, if ever, the kinds of socio-economic capacities required to fruitfully exercise their sexual and procreative power. Our circumstance is this: physical biology shifts into fully sexual and procreative gear by about the age of fifteen, if not sooner; but education, employment, family, and social location seldom enable any of us—most notably our men folk—to take up a socially and economically viable married life before the age of thirty.[11] Our educational and other institutions, as well as our habits and culturally prescribed norms, are very much retarded when measured against our biological schedule. Consequently, our churchly focus upon prescribing against premarital sex, when combined with our failure to prepare and encourage and empower our young people for earlier marriage, frequently places us in the utterly untenable position of prescribing that an entire biologically and emotionally urged population endure fifteen or more years of celibacy. Such a requirement is outrageous, badly out of synch with human biology, and therefore virtually impossible to achieve, entirely inconsistent with traditional African-American and African family/tribal patterns, and not in the least bit Christian. Therefore, our churchly prescription against premarital sex and procreativity must come with preparation for and encouragement of earlier marriage; otherwise, we are prescribing the ridiculous.

If sex cannot wait until age thirty (and it cannot; just ask any 15-year-old), then marriage cannot either (ask any of the older members of our congregations). Furthermore, lubricated latex, pills, implants, and sexual technique cannot adequately bridge the growing gap between biological readiness and socio-economic readiness. In order to strengthen and stabilize African-American family life, the traditional African and Christian linkage between sexuality, procreativity, marriage, and family must be mended. The gap between biological readiness for sexual activity and procreativity on the one side, and socio-economic-cultural readiness for married life on the other, must be closed, or at least narrowed to some reasonable breadth. This gap between biological readiness and social-economic-cultural readiness locates many of the most difficult problems pertaining to the deterioration of African-American families. In this gap, or chasm, one finds the highest concentrations of unwanted pregnancies, adult male-absent families, sexually transmitted disease, drug abuse, AIDS, and violent crime. The wider this gap, the more problematic, unstable, and fractured will family life be.

If we attempt to close this gap with motion only from the biological readiness side (i.e., combating adolescent pregnancy with prescriptions for abstinence and contraception), we encourage our youth to attempt to leap across a yawning chasm of social dislocation—fifteen or more years of sexual frustration or illegitimate sex—which is swallowing whole generations of our adolescent and young adult populations. Secular social ethics may prescribe condoms and contraceptive techniques and safe sex as a way of getting across this chasm; but African-American churches, by reason of our traditional commitment to the idea that sexual activity should be bounded by marriage and family, are not able to employ sexual instruments and techniques in this way. Instead, we are obliged to call for greater closure from the socio-economic-cultural side. If we know from the biological clock that sexual and procreative drives are in full gear at age x, then, according to traditional African-American folk wisdom, the responsible thing to do is to be prepared, working, and otherwise appropriately situated by no later than, if not before, the age of x. If we wish to continue with integrity the tradition of prescribing against premarital sex and procreativity, we must also take up the old-time tradition of preparing for and encouraging earlier marriage.

Of course those of us who are less old-fashioned and more "modern" in our thinking are likely to reject the idea of earlier marriages on the grounds that younger people are less "mature" and less able to take up the responsibilities of fully independent adult existence. But from a more traditional point of view, a younger couple's inability to be fully independent is not a call for them to forgo being a married couple; instead, it is a call for the surrounding community to be more supportive. The extended family, the church, and the surrounding community are called upon to provide support and empowerment for those who need such support.

The idea that a couple must be fully independent of family and community support in order to be married is a new and very untraditional idea. Only in recent generations has this idea come to prevail, and the experience of these recent generations indicates that it is not a good idea. Experience has taught us that this idea leads to postponed marriages, and to nonmarriages, but it seldom leads to greatly postponed sexual activity or to sexual abstinence. Generally, postponed marriages do not lead to postponed sexual involvements; instead, postponed marriages lead to increased and prolonged temptation to engage in premarital and extramarital sex. Those of us who are thereby burdened with opportunity to develop the swinging habits of the single life find that such habits, once acquired, are difficult to break. Obviously, it would make for more stable marriages and family life if we had never developed such habits to start with. Accordingly, in regard to the view that younger people are, by virtue of being younger (less "mature"), less able to keep marital vows, it is more likely that closed and committed relations are very natural and more easily learned by those who have had less opportunity to acquire the contrary experiences and habits of our more "mature" generations. While it is not modern, it is surely traditional, African, and Christian to insist that individuals who are sexually active should, from the very beginning of that activity, if not sooner, have that activity circumscribed by a marital covenant.

Our churches can and should take the lead in encouraging and empowering our people to take up these traditional social habits. Where marriage has failed to precede sexual activity, we must bring back shot-gun weddings, but we must replace the shot-guns with instruments of empowerment, support, and opportunity. Thus, we who, on account of our traditional and Christian commitments, must preach marriage, must also preach empowerment. Moreover, we must break such bread as will contribute to empowerment and opportunity for fruitful multiplication in marriage and family.

Thus, when we engage in social ethical reflection with and for public policy communities in a way that is consistent with the philosophy of black power and the tradition of independently empowered African-American churches, our coalition agenda is this: given that we wish to strengthen and stabilize African-American families rather than simply cutting the birthrate in black communities, let us break such bread as will prepare, enable, empower, and encourage African-American readiness for socially and economically viable married life at considerably younger ages and with much greater frequency than is currently the norm.

We need family planning programs that are genuinely about planning families, and this includes marriage counseling. (It is well known that presently, most "family planning" clinics in black neighborhoods are hardly, if at all, concerned with planning families; instead, they are primarily contraception distribution centers.) We believe that the arts of marriage and parenting and work and "home economics" need to be learned on a schedule no less accelerated than sexual/procreative capacities. Those who are able to be a parent ought to have learned by that age how to be, and how not to be, a parent. In a society such as ours, where this almost never happens, one must conclude that established generations have failed to provide adequate nurture, education, and support to coming generations.

To be sure, we may even go so far as to say we are actively miseducating coming generations. We are teaching coming generations that they should not marry until they have achieved the kind of socio-economic status that can hardly be achieved until fifteen years on the other side of puberty. We regularly teach that prior to marriage, one should have college and graduate degrees, a red brick house with a two-car garage containing two cars, a secure professional job, money in the bank, and more than a little experience ("shopping around") with a variety of prospective mates. These informal stipulations regarding the conditions that must be satisfied prior to marriage, in combination with the relative economic disadvantage of black males, have had the effect of dramatically reducing the marriage rate among our younger generations. The education and socialization that encourage present and coming generations to behave in ways that are so badly out of phase with human biology are socially dysfunctional. The result of this socially dysfunctional upbringing for African-Americans in the U.S.A. is that presently we are more likely than ever not to marry at all. When we do marry, we tend to marry at older rather than younger ages. And if, belatedly, we do marry, we are more likely than ever to separate and divorce, and less likely than ever to remarry.[12]

When, as is characteristic of our present circumstance, biological readiness is frustrated by social habits and structures of unreadiness, this contributes to the destabilization of family life. In order to strengthen and stabilize black family life, we must develop social institutions and habits of thought and deed that will prepare and empower our people for marriage and viable family life at higher rates and at considerably younger ages. Therefore, in addition to comprehensive bread-breaking socio-economic policies, such as are recommended by William Julius Wilson and the National Urban League, we see the need to bring obviously retarded educational institutions and social structures into phase with biological reality.

For those whose concern with stabilizing African-American birth rates is motivated by concern with global population pressures, it is important to remember that, as King pointed out, poverty tends to yield higher birthrates, and that therefore the best way to reduce global population growth is by contributing to the growth of global prosperity (WDWGFH pp. 177–78). Accordingly, I maintain that increasing the socio-economic resources that contribute to stable family life, rather than increased recourse to premarital contraception and abortion, is the better way to stabilize and strengthen black families in the U.S.A. and elsewhere.[13]

Let us then employ religious, social, educational, economic, political, and other resources to empower the people to marry young, to stay married until parted by death, and to enjoy viable and procreative family life. We seek, through the social ethic of breaking bread, to empower all the people, so that all may multiply fruitfully.

WAR ON DRUGS AND CRIME

It became characteristic of liberal social ethical reflection in the 1980s to insist that government and other public policy communities, including the military, should declare and wage "war" against the use and distribution of selected "controlled substances" or drugs. This prescription is also characteristic, perhaps even more characteristic, of conservative social ethical reflection in the 1980s and earlier. Moreover, both liberal and conservative public policy analysts agree that "drug-related" activity, aside from being a crime in itself, contributes to the increase of other criminal activity. To be sure, it is now widely conceived that the largest part of war against crime should consist of war against drugs, and also that both public and private sectors, including the work place, should join this war. While declarations of war on drugs and crime do not distinguish liberals from conservatives, they are sufficiently characteristic of liberal agenda to require our attention when we reflect upon the prospects for liberal coalition efforts.

To date, there is little to no sustained systematic reflection upon precisely this aspect of liberal agenda from the perspective of black power philosophy, or from the perspective of black theology. But the whole African-American community in the U.S.A. is acutely aware of the presence of drug and drug-related criminal activity in our communities; and hardly any sociological description of the African-American circumstance in the 1980s fails to mention these matters. Furthermore, numerous major African-American organizations along with many of our churches are increasingly concerned about drug abuse (alcohol, tobacco, cocaine, especially "crack" cocaine, heroin, etc.) and related social dislocations.

Clearly, Afro-America shares concern with, and suffers greatly from, abusive drug use and criminal activity. However, from our perspective it appears that many current and impending versions of warring against drugs and crime amount to war against black and colored people. Our experience of war on drugs and crime has been one of increased suffering and oppression. In addition to suffering the pains, which are a direct and physiological result of drug abuse and addictions, including the spread of disease, most notably AIDS, we also suffer from the loss of terribly large numbers of our people, especially our young males, to prisons and other socially debilitating facilities.

Federal and state prisons, and other correctional facilities, contain populations in which black and colored people, especially young black males, are highly and disproportionately represented.[14] While one might argue, wrongly, that the explosive growth of the black and colored prison populations protects upper- and middle-class interests from the crimes of lower- and underclass types who are disproportionately black and colored, it would be more difficult, perhaps impossible, to argue that such circumstances improve the public safety in lower- and underclass neighborhoods.[15] Indeed, black and underclass ghetto communities are experiencing the opposite effect.

When socially disadvantaged persons are sent to prison, they return further disempowered by even greater disadvantage. It is almost always the case that spending time in prisons and other so-called correctional facilities contributes to further social disadvantage. But the truth is even worse than this because these facilities seemingly always reinforce the kinds of habits of thought and action that issue in further recourse to violence, crime, and other socially debilitating behavior.

The fact that the prevailing structures of criminal incarceration are places where people increase in the knowledge and habits of homicide is indicated in the fact that inmates frequently describe their circumstance by saying they are in "gladiator school." Lawrence Gonzales's essay "Welcome to Gladiator School" (*Notre Dame Magazine*, vol. 17, no. 4, Winter 88/89) makes precisely this point when he quotes an inmate at the infamous Cook County, Illinois, Jail as saying, "If you don't know how to fight when you come here, you'll know how when you leave" (WGS p. 33). Gonzales says, "Prisons exist to serve as a wall between two classes, with a shuttle system to the ghetto. And the lesson taught behind the wall is simple: be bad or be dead" (WGS p. 1). The federal and other government structures, which operate a massive shuttle system into and out of our underclass communities, take in people who are poor and oppressed, and sometimes violent and criminal. They are then further oppressed, and further schooled in violence and crime, and then returned to our communities, not corrected or rehabilitated, but socially debilitated and empowered with greater capacity for, and greater need to resort to, crime and violence. Far more often than not, the structures of criminal incarceration yield a product that is worse off and more worrisome than the one it received. The multiplication of gladiator schools contributes to the increase of violent and criminal individuals in our communities.

Prisons produce gladiators. Increasing numbers of black males and others with experience in "gladiator school" means increasing numbers of gladiators in our communities. More gladiators yield more violence and crime, and more crime yields more gladiator schools graduating even more gladiators, and so on. This positive feedback loop is destroying underclass black communities and families throughout the U.S.A. As we experience it, this is not war against drugs and crime; it is a violent and criminal assault against our communities and families. Therefore we oppose the growth of this feedback loop, which is commonly referred to as "war" on drugs and crime.

From the perspective of black theology, including as it does our churchly and religious heritage, we prefer breaking bread to making war. In accordance with our ethic of breaking bread, we prefer policies of social empowerment over policies of imprisonment and extended gladiator training. In addition to our religious commitment to the ethic of breaking bread, we also recognize that policies of increased imprisonment are more costly than policies of increased empowerment. For example, the cost of keeping an individual in prison for a year is greater than the cost of sending an individual to college for a year.[16] Utilitarian considerations and, more decisively, our experience and religious ethic combine to suggest that the multiplication of gladiator schools or prisons is not a fruitful or righteous social policy.

Let liberal social ethics be advised: when "family planning" translates into a simple assault upon black birth rates rather than into planning socially viable families, and when "war on drugs/crime" translates into increased imprisonment and oppression rather than into an increase in alternative possibilities, then the ground for mutually beneficial coalition efforts is in serious jeopardy.

Where bread is not broken, God is not served, and the people are not free and empowered. From the perspective of black theology, the ethics of breaking bread—not the ethics of war and increased captivity—is the necessary ground for genuinely liberating coalition efforts.

NONVIOLENCE AS PART OF THE LIBERAL AGENDA

Another characteristic, though not distinctive, feature of many a white liberal coalition agenda is the insistence that blacks in the U.S.A. and elsewhere, most notably in southern Africa, adopt a policy of nonviolence. Those who would have us adopt nonviolence should be told that if they wish us to pledge allegiance to nonviolent struggle, then they will have to make the same pledge. And they should be advised that we regard extended gladiator training, both in prison and in the military, as a violation of that pledge. If they force gladiator training upon our young ones through prison and military experience, and if they use the alleged "entertainment value" of violence to cultivate homicidal habits of thought among all who are reached by television, movies, and other mass media, then they cannot expect us to keep a pledge to nonviolence.

Presently, the material preconditions for keeping such a pledge do not exist. The conditions that would have to obtain in order to keep a pledge to nonviolence include a substantial decrease in gladiator training, a substantial reduction in the profit-oriented cultivation of homocidal fantasies, and a substantial reduction in the production and distribution of the instruments of homicide and war. King's philosophy of nonviolence is not restricted to the domestic arena; it also demands nonviolence of the nation states (WDWGFH p. 184). Accordingly, a mutual pledge to nonviolence consistent with King's philosophy must include "finding an alternative to war" and militarism (WDWGFH p. 181), and it must include, as Carmichael and Hamilton insist, a commitment to "preach non-violence in the white community" (BP p. 82).[17] Those of us who are genuinely committed to nonviolence must busy ourselves with creating social conditions that admit the possible growth of nonviolent habits of thought and deed, and that admit the possible growth of nonviolent populations. In the absence of such efforts, all talk of nonviolence is an obscenity.

NOTES

1. Franklin I. Gamwell, *Beyond Preference: Liberal Theories of Independent Associations* (Chicago: University of Chicago, 1984), seeks to provide liberal thinking,

particularly the reformed liberal thinking indebted to John Dewey, with a philosophical foundation that is consistent with the metaphysical and theological reflections of Alfred North Whitehead and Charles Hartshorne. See also Gamwell's "Happiness and the Public World: Beyond Political Liberalism" in *Process Studies*, vol. 8, no. 1 (Spring 1978), reprinted in John B. Cobb and W. Widick Schroeder, *Process Philosophy and Social Thought* (Chicago: Center for the Scientific Study of Religion, 1981).

2. Leroy Fitts's book, *A History of Black Baptists* (Nashville: Broadman Press, 1985), provides historical witness to the fact that, among black Baptists, the tradition of conceiving of ourselves as an African people is older than the tradition of conceiving of ourselves as American, and as U.S. citizens. Fitts points out that the first independent black Baptist missionary society in the U.S.A. was organized in Richmond, Virginia, by the Reverend Lott Carey and Collin Teague in 1815, and that it was called "the Richmond African Baptist Missionary Society" (p. 45). Fitts records that "in 1846, two other black Baptist churches were organized in the City of Richmond—the First African Baptist Church and the Second African Baptist Church" (pp. 45–46). And Fitts goes on to teach us about "the African Meeting House of Boston which was constituted in 1805" and about the "Abyssinian Baptist Church" founded in New York City in 1808, and that the "First African Baptist Church of Philadelphia was organized on June 19, 1809" (pp. 46–47). Moreover, Fitts does not fail to note that the separatist and independent black church movement in the U.S.A. started with Bethel African Methodist Episcopal Church of Philadelphia (p. 47).

3. For example, James H. Johnson, Jr., director of the Center for the Study of Urban Poverty and professor of geography at UCLA, is quoted as saying, "the unfair and unnecessary job competition represented by massive immigration must be curtailed" (*Dallas Morning News* editorial by Richard Estrada, Friday, June 16, 1989). Also, for reflection upon how changes in the U.S. economy impact the existence of black and colored urban populations, refer to "Economic and Social Dislocations" by Johnson and Melvin L. Oliver in *Urban Geography*, vol. 10, no. 5 (September-October 1989).

4. The unfavorable African-American "male marriageable pool index" is understood to be a function of high African-American male joblessness combined with a high black male mortality rate and a high black male incarceration rate. Wilson's study of this index reveals "a long-term decline in the proportion of black men, and particularly young black men, who are in a position to support a family" (TD p. 8). Wilson goes on to say that "black women, especially young black women, are facing a shrinking pool of 'marriageable' (i.e., economically stable) men" (TD p. 91).

5. Wilson reports that "black women have much higher separation and divorce rates than white women" and he reports "a higher rate of remarriage among white women" (TD p. 68). Also, Wilson notes that "just as important a factor in the declining proportion of black women who are married and living with their husbands is the increase in the percentage of never-married women. Indeed, ... the proportion of never-married black women increased from 65 percent in 1960 to 82 percent in 1980 for those ages fourteen to twenty-four and from 8 percent to 21 percent for those ages twenty-five to forty-four" (TD p. 68). Wilson attributes delayed marriage and lower rates of remarriage to "the influence of male joblessness" (TD p. 91).

6. "Female-headed" is best translated as "adult male-absent" in reference to

the absence of an adult male parent or the absence of his positive contributions to the socio-economic well-being of children and family. Wilson frequently speaks of "female-headed" households and families under the category of family "deterioration" (TD p. 250). The reader might be misled by this way of speaking and come to think that Wilson is engaging in neo-chauvinist thought according to which there is something inherently pathological about a household or family that is "headed" by a female. Actually Wilson is using the term "female-headed" in a way that is similar to Hill's usage—as largely interchangeable with "one-parent" or single-parent (SBA/89 p. 41). Here and in most liberal sociology, the term "female-headed" is used to describe single-parent families in which it is typically the male parent who is absent. For example, the term "female-headed" is not used to refer to a family in which both parents are present, and in which the female is "the head," whatever that may mean. It is, then, not female-headedness per se, but the absence of one of two parenting heads—usually the male—that is problematic.

7. Marian Wright Edelman's contribution to the Urban League's 1989 report focuses on the status of black children. She reports that in 1987 "nearly one-half (45.1%) of all black children were living in poverty" (SBA/89 p. 65). Also, see Edelman's book—*Families in Peril: An Agenda for Social Change* (Cambridge: Harvard University Press, 1987).

8. See Daniel P. Moynihan, *The Negro Family: The Case for National Action* (Washington, D.C.: Office of Policy Planning and Research, U.S. Department of Labor, 1965). Also, for more recent reflection by Moynihan, see "Family and Nation" (Cambridge, Mass.: Harvard University's Godkin Lectures, 1985).

9. For example: Marian Wright Edelman, *Families in Peril: An Agenda for Social Change* (Cambridge, Mass.: Harvard University Press, 1987); Nathan and Julia Hare, *The Endangered Black Family: Coping With the Unisexualization and Coming Extinction of the Black Race* (San Francisco: Black Think Tank, 1984); Thomas A. Parham and Roderick J. McDavis, "Black Men, An Endangered Species: Who's Really Pulling the Trigger?," in *The Journal of Counseling and Development*, vol. 66 (September 1987); Haki R. Madhubuti, *Black Men: Obsolete, Single, Dangerous?: The African-American Family in Transition* (Chicago: Third World Press, 1990); Robert Staples, "Black Male Genocide: A Final Solution to the Race Problem in America," *The Black Scholar: Journal of Black Studies and Research*, vol. 18, no. 3 (May/June 1987).

10. Wilson reports "a sharp drop in the rate of teenage childbearing among both blacks and whites since 1960," but that "the proportion of black teenage births that were out of wedlock increased from only 42 percent in 1960, to 63 percent in 1970, and then to a staggering 89 percent in 1983" (TD p. 28). Hill notes that between 1970 and 1985, the out-of-wedlock birthrate for black teenagers fell "from 90.8 to 79.4 per 1000 unmarried women age 15–19" (SBA/89 p. 53). So the rate of black out-of-wedlock teenage pregnancy is not exploding, but it is still, says Hill, four times greater than the rising white out-of-wedlock teenage pregnancy rate; and Hill projects that this will be "a major area of concern for blacks throughout the 1990s" (SBA/89 p. 53). Edelman notes that "the number of black babies born to unmarried black women is declining," but that the rate is still unacceptably high—"61 percent of all births to black women were out-of-wedlock" in 1986 (SBA/89 p. 68). Edelman attributes the high proportions of out-of-wedlock black pregnancies to the "combined statistical impact of fewer black marriages and a low birth rate among black married women" (SBA/89 p. 68).

11. In regard to the ability of most black men in the U.S.A. to take up viable married life before the age of thirty, it is important to take note of sociological data such as that offered by Robert Staples in his article, "Black Male Genocide: A Final Solution to the Race Problem in America," *The Black Scholar*, vol. 18, no. 3 (1987). Here Staples points out that "over 50 percent of black men under the age of 21 are unemployed. . . . Forty-six percent of black men between the ages of 16–62 are not in the labor force . . . 32 percent of black men have incomes below the officially defined poverty level" (p. 3), and that "54 percent of black males, 18–29 years old, are living with their parents" while others live with women on AFDC or go homeless (p. 9).

12. Wilson's studies reveal that blacks in the U.S.A. are increasingly less likely to marry (TD p. 68), that those of us who do marry tend to marry late, that we are more likely to divorce or separate, and less likely to remarry (TD p. 91). Also, Marian Wright Edelman reports that "in the black community, young marriages have declined dramatically" (SBA/89 p. 67). Edelman and Wilson find that unemployment and underemployment contribute significantly to this trend. Also see Robert Staples, "Beyond the Black Family: The Trend Toward Singlehood," *The Western Journal of Black Studies*, vol. 3 (Fall 1979).

13. The September 1989 "Rough First Draft" of *World Conservation Strategy for the 1990s*, prepared by the World Conservation Union, the United Nations Environment Programme, and the World Wide Fund for Nature, also recognizes the need to address population pressure by contributing to economic development. The September 1989 draft says: "The only sure way of stabilizing population is to achieve one of the goals of sustainable development: the survival and wellbeing of people. Once people's survival and wellbeing are reasonably secure, they want fewer children and are able to have the number they want. At the same time, providing people with forms of social security other than large numbers of children—and with the means to limit their families—is a condition for securing their survival and wellbeing. Thus the two strategies—reducing population growth and increasing economic development that meets the needs of the poorest people in the poorest countries—are mutually reinforcing" (p. 68).

14. Paul Glasser-Kerr reports that according to *The Sourcebook of Criminal Justice Statistics 1987* (Washington, D.C.: Hindelang Criminal Justice Research Center, 1988), in 1986 African-Americans were 45.3% of federal and state prison populations (p. 491, Table 6.21). Similarly, in *Prophetic Fragments* (Grand Rapids: Eerdmans/Trenton: Africa World Press, 1988) Cornel West cites Manning Marable's work in *How Capitalism Underdeveloped Black America* (Boston: South End Press, 1983) in saying "every year over 8 percent of all Afro-Americans are arrested (representing over 25 percent of all Americans arrested in a given year)" and that "almost half of all prisoners in the U.S. are black" (PF p. 65).

15. Thomas L. Shaffer explains in his essay—"Why We Have Jails," *Notre Dame Magazine*, vol. 17, no. 4 (Winter 1988/89)—that we have jails because "they make three-bolt realists rest easier in the suburbs" (p. 42). Also see Mark S. Fleisher, *Warehousing Violence* (Newbury Park, Calif.: Sage Publications, 1989).

16. According to Paul Glasser-Kerr's research under the title "University Costs vs. Prison Costs" (unpublished, 1989), "The cost of keeping a person in a state prison is much greater than the average cost of educating a person at a state university." Glasser-Kerr concludes that since the annual cost of keeping an individual in prison is $17,885, compared with $6,721 for a year in college, we should

prefer "educating rather than incarcerating." Also see Donald P. Lay's "Our Justice System, So-Called" in the *New York Times* (Monday, October 22, 1990). Lay is chief judge of the Eighth Circuit Court of Appeals, and in this article he concludes that "punishment is one thing, but our incarceration policies are wasteful and should be changed. Present policies breed further crime, dehumanize individuals and require gross expenditures of tax dollars needed for other purposes."

17. Here Carmichael and Hamilton are repeating the view of Malcolm X who held that whites who sincerely wish to enter into coalitions favoring nonviolence should "teach nonviolence to white people." See *The Autobiography of Malcolm X*, Alex Haley, ed. (New York: Ballantine Books, 1964/1973), p. 377.

BIBLIOGRAPHY

Carmichael, Stokely and Charles V. Hamilton. *Black Power: The Politics of Liberation in America*. New York: Vintage Books, 1967.

Edelman, Marian Wright. "Black Children in America." *The State of Black America 1989*. New York: National Urban League, 1989.

———. *Families in Peril: An Agenda for Social Change*. Cambridge: Harvard University Press, 1987.

Fitts, Leroy. *A History of Black Baptists*. Nashville: Broadman Press, 1985.

Fleisher, Mark S. *Warehousing Violence*. Newbury Park, Calif.: Sage Publications, 1989.

Gamwell, Franklin I. *Beyond Preference: Liberal Theories of Independent Associations*. Chicago: University of Chicago Press, 1984.

———. "Happiness and the Public World: Beyond Political Liberalism." *Process Studies*, vol. 8, no. 1 (Spring 1978); reprinted in John B. Cobb and W. Widick Schroeder, *Process Philosophy and Social Thought*. Chicago: Center for the Scientific Study of Religion, 1981.

Glasser-Kerr, Paul. "University Costs vs. Prison Costs." Unpublished, 1989.

Gonzales, Lawrence. "Welcome to Gladiator School." *Notre Dame Magazine*, vol. 17, no. 4 (Winter 1988/89).

Hare, Nathan and Julia. *The Endangered Black Family: Coping With the Unisexualization and Coming Extinction of the Black Race*. San Francisco: Black Think Tank, 1984.

Hill, Robert B. "Critical Issues for Black Families by the Year 2000." *The State of Black America 1989*. New York: National Urban League, 1989.

Johnson, Jr., James H., and Melvin L. Oliver. "Economic and Social Dislocations." *Urban Geography*, vol. 10, no. 5 (September-October 1989).

King, Jr., Martin Luther. *Where Do We Go From Here: Chaos or Community*. New York: Harper and Row, 1967.

Madhubuti, Haki R. *Black Men: Obsolete, Single, Dangerous?: The African-American Family in Transition*. Chicago: Third World Press, 1990.

Marable, Manning. *How Capitalism Underdeveloped Black America*. Boston: South End Press, 1983.

McKissick, Floyd. *Three Fifths of a Man*. Toronto: Macmillan, 1969.

Moynihan, Daniel P. "Family and Nation." Cambridge, Mass.: Harvard University's Godkin Lectures, 1985.

———. *The Negro Family: The Case for National Action*. Washington, D.C.: Office

of Policy Planning and Research, U.S. Department of Labor, 1965.
Munro, David A. (project director). *World Conservation Strategy for the 1990s* (provisional title, "Rough First Draft") prepared by the World Conservation Union, the United Nations Environment Programme, and the World Wide Fund for Nature, September 1989.
Newton, Huey P. *To Die For the People: The Writings of Huey P. Newton.* New York: Vintage Books, 1972.
Oliver, Melvin L., and James H. Johnson, Jr. "Inter-Ethnic Conflict in an Urban Ghetto: The Case of Blacks and Latinos in Los Angeles." *Research in Social Movements, Conflicts and Change: A Research Annual*, vol. 6. Greenwich, Conn.: Jai Press, 1984.
Parham, Thomas A., and Roderick J. McDavis. "Black Men, An Endangered Species: Who's Really Pulling the Trigger?" *The Journal of Counseling and Development*, vol. 66 (September 1987).
Shaffer, Thomas L. "Why We Have Jails." *Notre Dame Magazine*, vol. 17, no. 4 (Winter 1988/89).
Staples, Robert. "Beyond the Black Family: The Trend Toward Singlehood." *The Western Journal of Black Studies*, vol. 3 (Fall 1979).
———. "Black Male Genocide: A Final Solution to the Race Problem in America." *The Black Scholar: Journal of Black Studies and Research*, vol. 18, no. 3 (May/June 1987).
West, Cornel. *Prophetic Fragments*. Grand Rapids: Eerdmans/Trenton, N.J.: Africa World Press, 1988.
Wilson, William Julius. *The Declining Significance of Race*. Chicago: University of Chicago Press, 1978.
———. *The Truly Disadvantaged: The Inner City, the Underclass, and Public Policy*. Chicago: University of Chicago Press, 1987.
X, Malcolm. *The Autobiography of Malcolm X*, Alex Haley, ed. New York: Ballantine Books, 1964, 1973.

CHAPTER FIVE

Power to the People

Sociological Descriptions, Predictions, and Socio-Ethical Prescriptions for the Exercise of Black Power

In previous chapters we affirmed the need to engage in dialogue with other communities of social ethical reflection and to engage in coalition efforts with liberal, reformed liberal, social democratic, and other liberating communities. We affirmed the bread-breaking aspects of liberal social ethical reflection, and we rejected those items on the liberal coalition agenda that are inconsistent with our ethic of breaking bread. Our relation to God teaches us that the ethic of breaking bread is appropriate to every social location; and therefore we affirm the basic liberal conviction that public and other sectors of society ought to contribute to the well-being of all, including disadvantaged populations, and that government in particular has bread-breaking responsibilities. But we shall not have done the job that the philosophy of black power and the elder tradition of the black church revolution call us to do if we do not return to our more immediate question of how best to break the bread that we control. *In this chapter our purpose is to present black scholarly reflections from the 1980s upon the social ethical question that black power calls us to consider: What ought we African-Americans in the U.S.A. do with the resources that we control in order to contribute to the comprehensive empowerment of all the people?* In the next chapter we shall evaluate black power's social ethical views from the 1980s and black power's social ethical prescriptions for the 1990s and beyond from the churchly perspective of black theology. We shall also reflect on the social ethical question that black theology calls us to consider: What should our African-American religious congregations do in order to contribute to the comprehensive empowerment of all the people?

The philosophy of black power was not much spoken of in the U.S.A. during the 1980s, but there was no shortage of social ethical reflection that fell within its definition. The 1980s produced a goodly quantity of sociological descriptions of the African-American experience, predictions for dire future circumstances, and prescriptions for social action on the part of African-Americans to improve upon present and future circumstances. Insofar as a given social ethical reflection is about exercising the liberating power of black people to improve upon present and future circumstances, that reflection seeks to answer the question that the philosophy of black power calls us to consider, and accordingly, that reflection falls within the body of social thought we identify under the philosophy of black power.

THE WITNESS OF THE MUSIC

It has been the tradition of the black church revolution, and of the philosophy of black power, to describe our contribution to the struggle for freedom in terms of "breaking the chains" of slavery and oppression. Many of us recall very clearly that one of the most popular symbols for black power during the 1960s and 70s was the image of two strong black fists snapping an iron chain. In our churches the chain and the cross are our symbols for oppression. The breaking of chains and the resurrection are our symbols for liberation and salvation.

In 1986 the black seminarians at Perkins School of Theology offered a program under the theme "Strategies for Social Change: Helping to Break the Chains." One of the things we learned at this program was that the symbol of the chain needs to be interpreted and reinterpreted for each generation. The meaning of broken chains—that is, the meaning of freedom—depends in part upon the social location and the kinds of oppression endured by a given generation.

Vincent Harding's history of the African-American struggle for freedom—*There is a River: The Black Struggle for Freedom in America*—teaches us this same lesson. From Harding we learn that for the African who is newly chained to the deck of a slave ship anchored on a West African coast, the meaning of freedom is somewhat different than for the same African on a plantation in North Carolina. Harding says that while "struggle was inevitable" (TR p. 3), the path and goal of the struggle varied with social location, in this instance with distance from Africa (TR p. 15). Harding shows that from the very beginning of our encounter with slavery, "already it was evident that from place to place, time to time, and setting to setting, the nature of our struggle was to be transformed and the question reshaped" (TR p. 15). From Harding we learn that the meaning of freedom, and accordingly the goal and path of the struggle, is, in large part, a function of social location.

Therefore, insofar as we seek to help break the chains, we must decipher the meaning of the symbol of the chain for our generation and our social location. We must ask ourselves: What kinds of shackles are these? What social structures and habits confine us here and now? What form does oppression take in the 1990s? In short, we must engage in social analysis.

James H. Cone's essay, "What is the Church?" in *Speaking the Truth: Ecumenism, Liberation, and Black Theology*, maintains that in order to define the church and its mission we must have recourse to social analysis. According to Cone, social analysis and doctrine, not doctrine alone, are essential resources for ecclesial and theological reflection.

Our social analysis of the chains that bind us includes considerable attention to formal academic social scientific reflection, as well it should. But our African-American and religious heritage empowers us to consider additional and, for us, utterly essential resources. Before further consideration of social scientific resources, let us consider an alternative and indigenous resource.

In the land that was once part of the black African empire of ancient Egypt, a land that has been called Canaan, then Judah and Israel and Palestine, in this once called "promised land" in greater North Africa, there is a city that is now venerated and rightly claimed by Christians, Jews, and Muslims alike—the city of Jerusalem. In the holy city of Jerusalem there is a wall, actually the standing remains from a stone wall that was pulled down when Roman soldiers destroyed Jerusalem in 70 C.E. This piece of the ancient wall of Jerusalem is now called "the wailing wall." The wailing wall is so named because this is where Jews come to cry, to grieve, and to wail before God. If, like God, we could hear and know the wailing at this wall, we would be well-informed about the pains and sufferings of Jewish people.

In the forcefully occupied land that was once wrongly called India, then called New World, now called America, there are Africans and descendants of Africans who have no "wailing wall." But with us, wailing—that is, the emotional articulation of pain and suffering—has become a cultural art form. The spirituals and the blues and the wail of Parker, Coltrane, and Miles, these are our wailings at the wall.[1] Traditionally, African-American music has been an indigenous folk articulation of our social circumstance. If we would be well-informed about the chains that inhibit African-American freedom, then we would do well to listen to this folk wailing at the wall.

The spirituals are about redemption and the salvation that comes with the acceptance of God's redemptive activity even in the face of severely difficult circumstances. Our spirituals affirm that, no matter how debased our existence, no matter how great the sufferings of slavery, oppression, and death, our existence has a value that is infinitely greater than its commodity relation to the structures of exploitation and oppression. Our spirituals affirm that the source of this value rests ultimately in our value to God. The blues are secular and nonreligious expressions of pain and suffering. While they seldom make explicit appeal to God, they nonetheless exhibit a faith that pain and suffering have a value and meaning that can be received, appreciated, and valued by others.

Spirituals, blues, gospel, jazz, and other traditional African-American art forms transmit expressions of our joys and pains, of our liberation and oppression, across land and sea, and across generations. Many of us have learned as much and more about the pains and joys, oppression and liberation, of our neighbors and forebears from these traditional sources as from any other.[2]

If we listen carefully to the lyrics, to the words, of the blues, and of soul music, and of more recent popular music such as rap, disco, go-go, new jack swing, funk, and the like, we would hear concern with many of the pains and "social dislocations" that characterize the day-to-day experience of African-Americans. Attention to these resources will force us to reflect further upon the problematic circumstance and crisis of African-American family life.

From the perspective of the African-American church, the most striking feature of much traditional secular African-American music, and of nearly all contemporary secular popular-urban African-American music in the U.S.A., is its inordinate fixation upon "love-life." Reverend Jesse Jackson, Minister Louis Farrakhan, and others have observed that our more popular music displays a socially dysfunctional and wholly irreligious conception of love. Here "love" almost always means romance and recreational sex. Moreover, far more often than not, love refers to sexual involvement outside marriage, or in violation of marital unions, and almost wholly without regard for procreative-family-cross-generational or social obligations. Love is conceived almost exclusively in terms of recreational sex between uncommitted or falsely committed individuals who are forever threatened, bedeviled, and oppressed by unstable, broken, and illicit affairs.

Listen to Tom Joyner in Chicago or to Dr. Rock in Dallas, to the Electrifying MoJoe in Detroit, to Daddy O in North Carolina, to Jivin Jimmy in Houston, to John R. in Nashville, or to the Quiet Storm in the District, and elsewhere. Listen to the prime time programs—"Power," "Foxy," "Kiss," "Strong Song," "Thunder Storm," "Traffic Jam," "Jamz," and the like—of virtually any major urban radio station that caters to young and middle-aged African-Americans. Listen to the words in the music on Don Cornelius's nationally televised "Soul Train." Listen to the words in the songs and watch the images in the music video shows on Black Entertainment Television (BET). Take ten songs in a row. Listen to the words, watch the video images, and see if this obsession about love-life does not apply to seven, eight, nine, or maybe even all ten songs.[3] Pick up any *Jet Magazine* published in the 1980s. Look at the top twenty singles list. See if you can find two songs in any top twenty listing that speak of love in ways that do not imply or specify this irreligious and socially dysfunctional conception of love. The point is this: the perennial theme of popular-urban African-American secular music is the fractured, broken, and problematically sexed love-life of our young and middle-aged population.

Above all else, this music is about the joy and pain, more the pain, and risk and satisfaction and frustration of recreational sex/"love-life." Denzel

Washington voiced disapproval of our music's near exclusive focus on this one theme in the song "Pop Top 40" in Spike Lee's movie *Mo' Better Blues*. Here Denzel Washington says, "what the world needs now is not another love song."

If we take seriously the wailing in the discos and from the boom-boxes and ghetto-blasters that are everywhere in our communities, the witness of our most popular secular music brings us easily to the conclusion that the problems of dysfunctional love-life and the high levels of anxiety and emotional violence between African-American men and women are among the most urgent difficulties of our present circumstance. The secular music that is now most popular among African-Americans in the U.S.A. testifies that the chain that binds us most severely in our most immediate day-to-day struggle is appropriately named in terms of contentious, unstable, and problematic interpersonal relationships and sexual linkages.

African-American social scientists have not been altogether unattentive to the relationship between our music and our problems in male-female-family relations. For instance, in 1979 James B. Stewart published "Relationships between Black Males and Females in Rhythm and Blues Music of the 1960s and 1970s." He described his article as "an exploratory investigation of the functionality of Rhythm and Blues music in Afro-American culture, specifically emphasizing the treatment of Black male-female relationships and familial formation in Rhythm and Blues music" (p. 186). Stewart found that in the 1960s our music favored traditional and popular American notions of romance, but with "little appreciation of the extent to which social, political, and economic forces can present barriers to romantic love"; and that in the 1970s our musical themes exhibited "a rejection" of the 1960s romanticizings (p. 186). Stewart went on to argue that, with the help of technological advances in the studio, the music industry was coming to exert so much control over the content of our music "that there will be less chance in the future that Black Rhythm and Blues will be as good a barometer of shared perspectives in the community as had been the case in the past." Stewart warned us of the dangerous "mind-boggling" potential that our music would become a white controlled marketing instrument, which shapes the values we live by in unfortunate ways, and he prescribed that it was "imperative" that we take steps to regain control of our music (p. 195).[4]

At the end of the 1970s Stewart saw that we were losing control of the content of our music and that this had potential for contributing to habits of thought that would increase male-female schism. Now, looking back on the 1980s, we see that Stewart's prediction was correct, and that he was then and remains now correct in warning that if we fail to exercise more righteous black power in this area, we can expect an even more difficult future for our male-female-family relations.

Some of us believe our music is more than merely a reflection of generally problematic love-life. We believe that during the 1980s our most widely marketed popular-urban music was actually contributing to the increase in such problems. As Stewart had warned in 1979, during the 1980s our music came under the near total control of Anglo-American business interests. Presently this music relentlessly presents schismatic and socially dysfunctional visions of love, love-life, and male-female relations. We believe that training our minds, particularly young minds, in such habits of thought cannot do other than contribute to similar habits in our deeds. This is severely dysfunctional wailing. To the extent that we are correct, the social ethical implication is that we need to do something righteous about our music.

Spike is right. We need mo' better blues. We need to start asking moral and social ethical questions about our music. Quincy Jones hinted at such inquiry in his recording of "What Good is a Song?" Here we are told that "if a song cannot take you higher, then it's not good enough to sing." If we understand "higher" to mean the kind of religiously "higher ground" that Stevie Wonder sings of, the point would be that a song that does not soothe, heal, enlighten, educate, worship, or empower is not good enough to sing. We need to sing different songs, so as to teach this and coming generations to conceive of love and love-life in ways that are explicitly inclusive of enduring family-tribal-socio-economic-cross-generational and procreative relations.

Even if, however, we refuse to take our music's determinative power so seriously as to insist that it actually contributes to unstable interpersonal relationships, we must still grant that our music, like the wailing at the wall, expresses the pain of problematic social relations known to almost all of us. But unlike the wailing at the wall, our popular music is very much filtered by marketing and profit-enhancing industries that are largely controlled by Anglo-American business interests. Here the profit-enhancing concern is with cultivating our consumer instincts rather than pointing the way to higher ground and empowerment. We have not failed to observe, for example, that many of the political protest and social consciousness themes that once characterized the music of Norman Whitfield, the Temptations, Stevie Wonder, and others have been screened out or displaced in favor of even greater concern with material consumption and recreational love-life. While we do not believe that the undeniable influence of media and marketing interests fully account for the level of fixation upon recreational love-life in our music, nonetheless the admitted contributions and influences of the music industry are such as might compel us to seek less altered data. Let us then consult the testimony of the African-Americans who listen to, buy, and dance to this music. Let us consult the witness of the people.

THE WITNESS OF THE PEOPLE

Nathan and Julia Hare are leading African-American sociologists who are very attentive to the witness of our people. Their socio-scientific instruments are designed to register the way in which African-Americans describe the circumstance of African-Americans. In their book, *The Endangered Black Family: Coping With the Unisexualization and Coming Extinction of the Black Race*, the Hares begin with an introduction called "For a Better Black Family." The very first sentence reads:

> The most talked about, but least understood, subject among black Americans today is black male-female conflict. [EBF p. 7]

They go on to speak of the problem of "black male-female schism" and of "the displaced power struggle that presents itself between the black male and the black female" (EBF p. 18) as an immediate threat to black family life in the U.S.A. Here we learn that African-Americans frequently describe the instability of African-American families in terms that are like those in our music—that is, in terms of male-female mistrust, anxiety, schism, and conflict.

To their credit, when Nathan and Julia Hare listen to the witness of black people, they pay due attention to the testimony of black women. When they offer prescriptions for liberation and empowerment, they are fully attentive to the status of black women. Their studies indicate that the black woman's greatest and most pressing lamentation is about black men:

> The black woman's greatest cry, if you will only talk to her sometimes and listen, is that she too often lacks a strong black male to stand beside her. She feels impelled too often to serve as the "backbone" of her family and to fulfill the formidable obligation of "both mother and father" to her children. [EBF p. 30]

> A black woman in this society is almost unanimously inclined to relate her main difficulty to her compensation for the failure of the black male. She sees her problem as the black man—her need to help him, his tendency to leave her alone with the children, ... the loss of a husband or a father or both. [EBF p. 82]

> These findings would suggest that more than half of the black female adult population of the United States lives in a condition of psychological distress rather than psychological well being. Black women will tell you, if you listen to them, that much of all the stress they ever feel is fired in them, one way or another, by the behavior of the black male as a social type and, in particular, by their personal mates. [EBF p. 118]

> She not only faces a depletion of the black male marital supply by jails and prisons, addiction, homicide, polluted occupational situations, unemployment, underemployment and the dereliction of psy-

chological escapism; she also must contend with the decimation of the young male's ability to hold to his romantic and sexual commitments today. [EBF p. 119]

An honest examination of the black family would reveal perhaps the most painful problem of the black woman—that somebody is depleting, alienating, stealing and otherwise threatening ... her male. [EBF p. 30]

The Hares report that black women understand the crisis of the black family to be, in large part, about black men, about the relative nonavailability of marriageable black men, about the deficient socio-economic resources of available black men, about the behavior of black men, and about conflict and disagreement with and over black men.

With regard to the testimony of black men, the Hares report:

Black males almost unanimously see the hardest thing about being a black man as revolving around economic and occupational problems—that is, making it in the system. [EBF p. 82]

Thus, while black women throughout our society are lamenting the relative nonavailability of socially advantaged and marriageable black men, black men are complaining first about their declining access to labor-market and other socio-economic resources, and secondly about their relations to black women and families.

The Hares perceive that these two partly gender-specific cries are strongly related in that the socio-economic disempowerment of black males deprives black women of access to socio-economically advantaged black men.[5] The disadvantaged and destabilizing social circumstance of African-Americans in the U.S.A. has, according to the Hares, contributed to an escalating and severely dysfunctional warfare between black men and women. The relative socio-economic disadvantage of the black man, in combination with the black woman's own socio-economic disadvantage, makes it difficult for a black woman and a black man to be advantages to each other.

The Hares report that in addition to the black man's increasing inability to exercise the kinds of socio-economic power required to fulfill traditional family obligations, there is—in the wake of new morality, gay liberation, feminist and androgynous trends—increasing confusion and disagreement concerning the proper social behavior and roles of males and females. As socio-economic disadvantage increases, as it becomes less possible for black men to form viable, enduring, and mutually advantageous socio-economic relationships with black women, and as confusion about gender-specific roles increases, the opportunity for black male-female conflict is greatly increased.

The Hares tell us that both male and female African-Americans in the U.S.A. report widespread and high levels of gender conflict. They describe the present African-American circumstance in terms of an escalating and severely dysfunctional warfare between black men and women.

Thus are many black men and women hateful partners in a harrowing dance. [EBF p. 89]

HATEFUL PARTNERS IN A HARROWING DANCE! This in turn contributes to the splintering of black families.

As I have indicated, our music testifies that our male-female relationships are perpetually unstable and problematic, though not so consistently untrusting and hateful as reported by the Hares. But, as I have also indicated, the witness of our music is media-filtered and romanticized. And as Stewart predicted, our music is becoming so much out of our control that it is apt to be an increasingly unreliable barometer of African-American social reality. It may then be that the Hares are closer to the truth, especially in that the witness they consult—statistically significant samples of African-American individuals—is a more indigenous African-American witness than is media-filtered and promoted popular music.

The Hares' attention to the liberation of black women is clearly distinct from, and somewhat at odds with, the prevailing white feminist liberation agenda. In fact, it is their view that white feminist liberation movements, along with gay liberation movements, have actually exacerbated the male-female conflicts and associated fragmentation of families that characterize African-American experience. They identify antimale feminism, antimaternal feminism, the general romanticizing of ephemeral relationships, alienation of parent-child relations (EBF p. 21), ultra-permissive child rearing, romanticizing of single parenthood, unisexism and unisexualization, homosexuality, lesbian experimentation, compensatory celibacy, diverse forms of sexual anorexia, and certain forms of experimentation with polygamy, as trends that contribute to the "further splintering or nuclearizing of the family unit" (EBF pp. 63–67). In short, they argue that white feminist and gay liberation movements add to the growing confusion regarding gender roles and expectations, and this exacerbates male-female conflicts among African-Americans.

Moreover, the Hares maintain that white feminist liberation movements have actually contributed to the increasing socio-economic disadvantage of black males in that large numbers of affluent white housewives in search of self-expression and personal satisfaction are taking jobs and other resources that might otherwise have been available to those in greater need—most particularly black men (EBF p. 24):

Almost to the exact extent that the white female has entered the labor force the black male has been pushed out of it, with obvious consequences for black sexual and family relationships. [EBF p. 25]

> The future of the black female is accordingly with the black male, just as the future of the black male must be with the black female. The white female also attests to a common oppressor, but the white woman sleeps with her enemy. For better or worse, we must never forget, her oppressor is her father, her son, her husband, her lover; and they are bound by the umbilical cord of biology itself. [EBF pp. 93–94]

In short, the Hares believe that the white middle-class feminist agenda does not serve, and at times even subverts, the liberation and empowerment of black women and black families.

The Hares report that while white feminists are striving to break white patriarchy, black women and black families are suffering and lamenting the loss of stable black patriarchy:

> The black woman longs for a black man with strength and prominence, even the chance herself to be weak sometimes ... She senses what Kathleen Cleaver has called a "broken patriarchy," a phenomenon that was misnamed "the black matriarchy" by poetic sociologists of the post-Depression era, but it is a phenomenon ... of relative powerlessness of the black male, which is real by any other name and must be dealt with by black people. [EBF pp. 159-160]

The Hares find that from the perspective of African-American women and families, freedom must include such socio-economic empowerment as makes possible positive aspects of stable black patriarchy (EBF p. 150).

For the immediate future however, the freedom that includes improved male-female-family relations and stable black patriarchy is going to be difficult to come by. In chapter 13 of *The Endangered Black Family*—"Coping with Alienation in the Coming Bad Years"—the Hares predict that, in this regard, the coming years will be bad. We shall have to learn to cope with a social circumstance characterized by increasingly probable alienation in our male-female-family relations.

SOCIAL ETHICAL PRESCRIPTIONS

Our most credible sociological data indicate that African-American families in the U.S.A. are in trouble, that black families are fragmenting and splintering at catastrophic rates. The Hares point to contentious male-female relationships as the area of greatest schism. They describe our relationships as openly hostile, and it is their "general thesis" that the "relative oppression of the black male" is "a primary factor in black male-female relations" (EBF pp. 78–79). They point out that the socio-economic resources available to black males have been decreasing faster than for black women, and it is becoming less and less possible for black men to fulfill the positive roles expected of them—hence, the "broken patriarchy."

Thus, socio-economic disadvantage generally, and the socio-economic disadvantage of black males in particular, contributes to the destabilization of black male-female relations, and to the destablization of black families and tribes.

Accordingly, the Hares prescribe that we adopt a two-fold strategy—a strategy that addresses the structures of socio-economic disadvantage and directly addresses problematic male-female relations:

> We as a people must begin to recognize that our task is a two-fold strategy, to alter and improve our most intimate relations, and in turn our institutional life, to codify and unify, while in the process changing and preparing to change the entire social structure, knowing that there is no possibility of a free and healthy relationship in the fullest sense in an oppressive, morally decadent and amorphous society. But rather than fall victim to the old chicken or the egg see-saw, we will choose to face the oppressor on both fronts. [EBF pp. 168-69]

From the Hares' analysis we may discern that our contribution to the struggle to stabilize and improve African-American family life must have three parts. (1) There is the part to be played by African-Americans working in *coalition* with such others as will contribute to comprehensive socio-economic empowerment. (2) There is a somewhat exclusive *African-American effort* to remedy socio-economic disadvantage—a unilateral exercise of black power in the form of breaking the bread that we control so as to contribute to the socio-economic empowerment of the people. (3) There is a very much *more exclusively African-American effort* on the part of black males and females to heal the schisms that have grown between us in our most intimate relations.

Coalition Efforts to Remedy Economic Powerlessness

In the Hares' work, it is the very much more exclusively African-American effort to heal male-female-family schism that is attended to, but they do seem to share with William Julius Wilson, the National Urban League, and other liberal public policy advocates the basic liberal conviction that public/governmental and other sectors of society should contribute to the socio-economic well-being of all, including disadvantaged populations.[6] The Hares prescribe that "a program of mass employment and reconstruction other than in prisons and military camps is necessary if the black family is ever going to be restructured as a viable leverage in the quest for social and economic elevation" (EBF pp. 17–18). However, the Hares' view is distinguished from many a liberal public policy view in that they do not regard excessive focus on pregnancy prevention as positive. The Hares are concerned with increasing the possibility of fruitful multiplication rather than with impeding the possibility of simple multiplication. They favor genuine family planning (planning that favors the reproductive rights and child-rearing and family-formation rights of women and men) rather than planning not to be family via contraceptive instruments and techniques. The Hares also reject the assumption that the multiplication of gladiator schools—prisons and military experience—is fruitful social policy.

The Hares' analysis reveals that many liberal social policies exacerbate schismatic black male-female relations and further destabilize black families on account of the fact that such policies typically offer some, though inadequate, economic empowerment to black women and families (especially favored are women and families where the men are absent) while at the same time denying or failing to provide economic empowerment for black men. For example, for several generations AFDC (Aid For Dependent Children) and other welfare policies have favored homes in which men are absent to the neglect of and discrimination against homes in which men are present. Such policies have frequently meant that poor women and families were effectively required to live apart from their menfolk.

Also the Hares observe that in recent decades the labor-market resources available to black women have not suffered the rate of decrease that has obtained for black men:

> Our computations from The Social and Economic Status of the Black Population and the United States: An Historical View, 1970–1978, reveals that when we employ the concept of relativity (inasmuch as all things are relative), we discover that the black female is unique in having changed her relative full-time median income appreciably since mid-century. But—and here is the tragedy—she is also unique in having changed her relative suicide rate: and she has changed relative income and her relative suicide rates to about the same degree. [EBF p. 118]

Here the Hares are viewing the relatively high and increasing suicide rate of black women as an index of their relatively high and increasing anxiety levels caused in large part by the increasing socio-economic disempowerment of their black men and by the increasing scarcity of socio-economically advantaged black men.

The Hares compare the position of black women to that of white women in a way that indicates that the white feminist agenda has worked to the disadvantage of black women:

> The white man's full time median income, relative to the white woman's, has not changed since the onslaught of feminism; it is the black male who has lost relative ground, despite a brief flash in the piepan in between World War II and the current white feminist years. Feminism allowed the white man to keep his act together while he further alienated and distorted and confused black male/female relationships.

This trend in turn impacts upon and pulverizes the black male's relationships with the black woman which now are compounded by the ambiguities and rationalizations resulting from the ideals and rhetoric of an anti-male, even anti-maternal, white feminism. The white race has a woman problem; the black race has a woman problem and a man problem in that, unlike the white man, the black man is also oppressed. The white woman has only to raise herself to the level of her man. If the black woman moves up without a simultaneous escalation of the black male, she will compound her isolation and too often look around to find that there is no strong black man to stand beside her. [EBF p. 160]

So by this measure, the effect of white feminist advances in public policy and private sector employment practices has been to inadequately empower black women while further disempowering black men; and this has worked to the disadvantage of stable black male-female relations. What is needed is socio-economic empowerment for both males and females.

The socio-economic disempowerment of men relative to women is described by the Hares as a violation of "sociological law." They say that "within a patriarchal society, it is suicidal to elevate the oppressed [black] female's economic attainment without also raising the oppressed [black] male's economic condition" (EBF p. 118). In accordance with this sociological law, the Hares believe that the combined effect of increasing, though inadequate, empowerment of black women, on the one hand, and increased disempowerment of black men on the other, has contributed to increasing black male-female conflict and to unstable and fractured family life. While the Hares agree with the basic liberal conviction that public and other sectors of society ought to contribute to the socio-economic empowerment of all—including disadvantaged populations—they teach us that in our coalition efforts we should be mindful of the need to develop policies of socio-economic empowerment that, unlike many heretofore liberal policies, do not result in relative disadvantage for black males.

African-American Efforts to Heal Male-Female-Family Schism

The part of our contribution to the struggle to stabilize and improve African-American family life, which is most exclusively described under the category of black power, includes the effort to address directly one of the most obvious and distressing symptoms of continually increasing socio-economic disadvantage—male-female conflict and other breakage in African-American family relations. For the Hares, the problem of black male-female conflict is no merely docile and domestic concern. It is a matter of serious revolutionary significance. In "Revolution Without a Revolution: The Psychology of Sex and Race," Nathan Hare teaches us that a social movement that heals the breakage between African-American men and women and between African-American men and families can spell the difference between continued oppression and the possibility of liberation. Moreover, the Hares are consistent with the philosophy of black power in perceiving that the success or failure of the African-American struggle for comprehensive empowerment has important consequences for the global struggle. Nathan Hare has been quoted as saying:

> America is like a giant octopus with a body and many tentacles. The Afro-American lives inside the body; Third World societies encounter only the tentacles. Black Americans, then, are able to deliver the most decisive blows to make the system more humane. [RBF p. 15]

The blows that we would deliver in favor of freedom and empowerment could make a decisive difference for Third World communities suffering the grip of remotely controlled tentacles. But, as the Hares see it, we shall have to heal the schism that has grown between black males and females, and other breakage in family and tribal cohesion, before we shall be able to deliver even the most feeble of such blows. Accordingly, the Hares understand that our effort to heal black male-female schism is a matter of considerable significance to the global struggle for the liberation and empowerment of all the people (EBF pp. 136, 169, 187).

In regard to this aspect of black empowerment, in *The Endangered Black Family*, the Hares prescribe the following:

> We propose that we begin to establish black love groups (psychological workshops, group therapy) to begin to elevate black love groups to the status of a social movement reminiscent of, but by no means mimicking, the popularity of so-called encounter groups. ... In this way we can begin to iron out our differences and our difficulties and perhaps to arrive ultimately at a workable solution. ... We believe that through black love groups we may learn to love again (that is, to feel loved), to love ourselves, and therefore one another. [EBF p. 19]

The Hares believe that we African-Americans need to develop a social movement that includes workshops and group therapy sessions designed to heal conflicts between black males and females.

The Hares understand that another important way by which we might create possibilities for improved relations between black males and females is by improving upon the socialization of black boys. The Hares recommend that we develop "rites of passage" for African-American males. To this end, the Hares have published *Bringing the Black Boy to Manhood: The Passage*. In this little booklet (42 pages), the Hares offer psychologically informed instructions for developing ceremonial rites of passage designed to bring the black boy into manhood. Additionally, the Hares are currently preparing complementary instructions for black girls under the title *The*

Broken Patriarchy: Bringing the Black Girl to Womanhood: The Passage.
Jawanza Kunjufu is another African-American scholar who sees the need for a rites of passage movement aimed at bringing the black boy to manhood. Kunjufu maintains that our collective habits of socialization conspire against the well-being and empowerment of black children generally, and against the well-being and empowerment of black boys especially. In order to improve upon this circumstance, Kunjufu has published numerous texts that offer instruction regarding the development of rites of passage as well as other information pertaining to the development of more effective education and socialization for black boys and black children.[7] Kunjufu, then, agrees with the Hares in holding that the present circumstance of African-Americans in the U.S.A. demands that a liberating exercise of black power include vastly increased attention to the education and socialization of black youth, and of black boys in particular.

Kunjufu and the Hares are among many African-American scholars who believe that the movement toward black empowerment must include considerable focus upon problematic black male-female relations and other matters of family and tribe. To be sure, the Hares have recently edited a book, *Crisis in Black Sexual Politics*, which contains contributions from seventeen other scholars who have joined them in describing the present circumstance of African-Americans in the U.S.A. in terms of black male-female conflict and other difficulties in our family and tribal existence.[8] Here the Hares prescribe that we African-Americans must develop our own black family agenda, and that this agenda should include emphasis upon "the black woman's family rights" (CBSP p.168). The Hares along with the contributors to *Crisis in Black Sexual Politics* provide us with a social ethical analysis that calls us to exercise black power to strengthen and stabilize black family life by protecting and enhancing "productive rights for the black male and reproductive/family rights" for the black female (CBSP p. 168). Furthermore, the Hares agree with us in recognizing that "the problem with black teenagers is not so much that they are getting pregnant as they aren't marrying" (CBSP p. 12), and in recognizing that "a case could be made that the real pathology is in the extreme length of time that society has placed between physical and social puberty" (CBSP p. 12).

Other African-American social analysts have offered a similar emphasis. Delores P. Aldridge's "The Black Family: Socialization and Conflict" offers a review of sociological literature focusing upon black male-female relationships. She reports a general consensus to the effect that it is important that "black men and women address unsatisfactory interpersonal relationships by participating in personal growth and human relations group sessions" (BFSC p. 190). Aldridge also finds agreement that universities should "develop and include a course on male and female relationships as part of their general education curriculum" and that black national organizations should "place on their program agenda the issue of strategies for strengthening relationships between Black men and Black women" (BFSC p. 190).

Osei-Mensah Aborampah's "Black Male-Female Relationships: Some Observations" provides another helpful review of social ethical reflection by African-American scholars who describe the present circumstance of African-Americans in the U.S.A. in terms of high levels of conflict in black male-female relations and the relative disadvantage of black males. Aborampah says this literature indicates that the severely problematic aspects of black male-female relations are a function of "two major social forces: the impact of society and its major institutions on the one hand, and the influence of persons and groups with which individuals interact on the other" (BMFR p. 321). The social structural forces include a substantial sex ratio imbalance in the African-American population, structures of racism and sexism, and, in particular, income inequality and unemployment. The influences of persons and groups upon individuals include factors such as socialization, domestic stresses resulting from financial difficulties, and a male double standard according to which it is commonly held that "extramarital coitus" by husbands is not so unacceptable as the same behavior on the part of wives (BMFR p. 321).

In regard to sex ratio imbalance, Aborampah points to work by J. Jackson showing that the number of black males available to black women has been declining since 1950. More recently, in 1972, there were only 70 available black male adult singles per 100 black female singles nationally. Aborampah notes that Robert Staples has shown that in some geographic areas, there is only one black male for every five black females. Jackson has demonstrated, says Aborampah, "a causal relationship" between the persistence of this sex ratio imbalance and the prevalence of female-headed families (BMFR pp. 321–24).

In regard to income inequality and unemployment, Aborampah says this literature indicates that:

> Perhaps at the core of the problems in black dating and marital relationships is the perennial problem of jobs and adequate income to provide the material base for meaningful and satisfying relationships. [BMFR p. 324]

Aborampah refers us to work by Jessie Bernards and Robert Staples showing that financial and employment anxieties contribute to difficult interpersonal and marital relations (BMFR pp. 324–28).

In regard to socialization, Aborampah points to work by C.W. Franklin indicating that the socialization of black children yields "noncomplementary sex-role definitions that serve to tear the sexes apart" (BMFR p. 328). Aborampah also refers to work by Staples indicating that "the very same traits that the black female acquires and marshals in her career mobility efforts are the ones that make it very difficult for her to attract and hold a black man" (BMFR p. 329). Furthermore, Aborampah refers us to work by A. Billingsley showing that AFDC requirements have for many years forced low-income black mothers to choose "between a father in the home and money in the home" (BMFR p. 330). Aborampah also points out that Staples and others find that college-educated blacks are particularly victim of socialization that contributes to gender conflict (BMFR pp. 331-32).[9]

In regard to the social ethical prescriptions that characterize this literature, Aborampah reports that the scholars who describe the African-American circumstance in terms of problematic male-female relations typically call for a restructuring of the American economy so as to ensure full employment for all. A collection of such essays in *The Black Scholar* ("The Crisis of the Black Male," volume 18, number 3, May/June 1987), for example, is said to indicate "that if the public and private sectors of the American economy are not restructured to ensure full employment for all, the black male population in particular stands a good chance of being decimated" (BMFR p. 333). Aborampah's review teaches us that the African-American scholars who describe our present circumstance in terms of male-female conflict typically offer public policy recommendations that presuppose the basic liberal conviction that public and other sectors of society should contribute to the socio-economic empowerment of all—including disadvantaged populations. His review teaches us that they typically offer recommendations for self-help efforts—that is, they typically offer social ethical prescriptions that answer the characteristic question of the philosophy of black power—What must we black folk do among ourselves with the resources that are ours to control in our own communities in order to improve upon this circumstance?

Aborampah finds that we are frequently called upon to achieve "drastic alterations in the socialization of black males and females." The work of R. Staples, C.W. Franklin II, M.K. Asante, and Ann Hulbert are among his sources. Aborampah points to Ann Hulbert's call for efforts to influence the attitudes and motivations of our teenagers, and to Staples's stress upon the need to provide our young ones with adequate premarital preparation. Aborampah describes the social ethical prescriptions of this literature in terms of a "call for a new value system" or "a call for value revival" (BMFR pp. 334-35).

After having reviewed many of the important sociological studies focused upon problematic black male-female relations, Aborampah offers his own social ethical prescriptions for achieving a renewal of values within our communities. Aborampah prescribes "the institutionalization of transitional rites" or "rites of passage" as a "socialization technique" by which to reach black children and prepare them for harmonious male-female relations (BMFR pp. 336-37). He draws upon E.G. D'Aquili's reflections on the role of ritual, and upon Asante's view that "a breakdown of African transitional rites for boys and girls" is at the root of many of these male-female difficulties (BMFR p. 334). Aborampah prescribes that "blacks need to create socialization techniques, including transitional rites," and he calls upon black community leaders and intellectuals to create and sustain appropriate rites for black children (BMFR p. 339). (Moreover, Aborampah appreciates the religious, spiritual, and churchly aspects of value-reviving ceremonial rites. We shall return to this point in the next chapter.)

Aborampah, like the scholars described in his review of the literature of socio-scientific reflection upon problematic black male-female relations, and like the scholars described by Aldridge in her review of such socio-scientific literature, is like the Hares in recognizing the need for coalition efforts to work with public and other sectors to achieve such comprehensive transformations in the American economy as will produce full and equal employment and socio-economic empowerment. And, like the Hares, he calls for a specifically African-American effort at comprehensive transformations in the values, motivation, and social habits of our young ones. Along with Kunjufu, the Hares, and others, Aborampah prescribes that African-Americans develop ceremonial rites of passage and other socializing techniques by which to help our young ones learn what they must know in order to overcome the social forces that conspire to divide black males from black females and families.

Another reflection upon the problematic circumstance of African-American families in the U.S.A. in the 1980s, and which offers social ethical prescriptions for the liberating exercise of black power, is Marian Wright Edelman's "An Agenda for Empowerment" in *Essence* magazine. We recall having considered Edelman's contribution to the Urban League's 1989 report in our reflection upon prescribed liberal coalition efforts (chapter 3). While Edelman's contribution to the Urban League's 1989 report is addressed to the public policy community, her 1988 article in *Essence*, in accordance with the *Essence* audience—"The Magazine for Today's Black Woman"—is addressed primarily to middle-class black women and families. Therefore the social ethical prescriptions in the *Essence* article fall more fully under the philosophy of black power. Still, like most philosophers of black power, Edelman does not fail to prescribe items appropriate to coalition agenda.

As founder and president of the Children's Defense Fund, Edelman describes the African-American circumstance in terms of the well-being of children and infants, and accordingly, in terms of the well-being of their families. She says that "it is the worst of times for poor Black babies born in many inner cities around the country." "It is the worst of times for Black youths and young adults who are trying to form families without decent skills or jobs and without a strong value base. Young marriages have essentially ceased to exist in the Black community" (AE p. 66). Edelman prescribes:

> The Black middle class must begin to exert more effective and sustained leadership within and without the Black community on behalf of Black children and families—as personal role models and value instillers and as persistent advocates for national, state and local pol-

icies (funded policies) that ensure our children the health and child care, education, housing and jobs they need to become self-sufficient adults, form healthy families and carry on the Black tradition of achievement. [AE p. 66]

Edelman identifies nine items in her agenda for the empowerment of black children and families:

(1) Remember to teach children that Black folks have never been able to take anything for granted in America. ... Tell our children that they're not going to jive their way up the career ladder. They have got to work their way up—hard and continuously. ... (2) Teach our children the importance of getting a good education. ... (3) Tell them that forming families is serious business and requires a measure of thoughtful planning and economic stability. ... (4) Set goals and work quietly and systematically toward them. ... (5) Know the difference between substance and style. ... (6) Value family life. ... (7) Vote and use our political and economic power. ... (8) Remember your roots, your history and the forebears' shoulders on which you stand. And pass them on to your children and to other Black children. ... (9) Keep dreaming and aiming high. [AE pp. 66, 132–34]

In short, Edelman's agenda for empowerment is about what black people must teach black children and youth so as to achieve righteous value and character formation, and about black contributions to coalition efforts to develop national priorities with funding that favors babies and mothers over missiles and bombs (AE p. 134).

African-American Efforts to Remedy Economic Powerlessness

Edelman, Aborampah and many of the scholars in his review, Kunjufu, the Hares and the contributors to their work, and many others who are concerned with exercising black power to stabilize and improve African-American family life acknowlege the need to develop and contribute to liberating/bread-breaking national economic policies. In addition to affirming this aspect of liberal coalition agenda, they reflect at length upon the need for deliberate efforts from within African-American families and communities to heal broken relations, to form stronger relations, and to create improved possibilities for our young ones—including adolescents, children, infants, and the yet-to-be-born. Without developing the point, Edelman touches upon another part of our struggle to improve African-American family life when she prescribes that we use our "economic power" (AE p. 133).

The use of economic resources to improve upon the circumstances of disadvantaged African-Americans and other disadvantaged populations is usually, at least in the sociological literature, discussed in terms of encouraging the development of national coalition and public policy efforts to remedy economic powerlessness. But even when public policy and other communities decline to contribute to our economic empowerment—as was characteristic of the 1980s—we must still continue with our own independent efforts to foster the growth of black economic power. The specifically African-American effort to contribute to economic empowerment is an aspect of the black power agenda developed by Harold Cruse under the label of "plural but equal."

Professor Harold Cruse, of the department of history and Afro-American studies at the University of Michigan, offers a historical account of how African-Americans came to the present circumstance in his book, *Plural But Equal: Blacks and Minorities in America's Plural Society*. Cruse's analysis is characterized by an unrelenting insistence upon the need to develop a specifically African-American platform—"a politics of black ethnicity" (p. 356)—as the precondition for successful coalition efforts to improve the economic position of African-Americans.

Cruse argues that the traditional civil rights leadership style, as represented by the NAACP and the National Urban League, has failed to address "the central problem of black people in the aggregate—economic powerlessness" (PBE p. 360). Cruse characterizes traditional civil rights leadership as being based upon a philosophy of "noneconomic liberalism." Noneconomic liberalism has failed because it all but ignores the problem of economic powerlessness.

Here Cruse draws upon the basic economic philosophy of Booker T. Washington, Marcus Garvey, and the later views of W.E.B. DuBois. Most of us remember DuBois for his leadership in the NAACP, and for his disagreements with Washington and Garvey. But Cruse points out that in 1934 DuBois broke with the NAACP on account of its philosophy of noneconomic liberalism. In this regard, in his later years, DuBois's views moved more in the direction of Garvey and in the direction of Washington's emphasis upon economic empowerment (though not in the direction of Washington's accommodation to de jure segregation).[10] According to Cruse, the NAACP, because it was imbued with a white philosophy of noneconomic liberalism, was unable to provide leadership, which included economic empowerment in its agenda. Instead the NAACP restricted itself to policies favoring integration and assimilation based upon constitutional and legal protections, which failed to include provisions for economic empowerment.

Cruse points out that Washington, Garvey, and DuBois came to realize that the failure to pursue economic empowerment was a debilitating aspect of traditional African-American leadership. Cruse affirms that DuBois and Garvey were correct in criticizing the traditional civil rights leadership for its failure to, in the words of DuBois, "envisage any direct action of Negroes themselves for the uplift of their ... depressed masses" (PBE p. 207). Similarly, Cruse notes that Marcus Garvey had "condemned Afro-American leaders precisely because they were, in his view, committed to no racial goals but assimilation" (PBE p. 211). In other words, the traditional civil rights leadership was very much concerned with what others—particularly the federal government—should do for the uplift of African-Americans; but it had little, beyond the pursuit of integration, to offer in regard to what African-Americans should do for their own uplift. Cruse identifies these failures as a "crisis in Negro leadership," and Cruse maintains that this crisis is with us even now.[11]

In an effort to help remedy this crisis, Cruse calls for a "new-style political leadership" free of the liabilities of noneconomic liberalism, and free of utter dependence upon expired New Deal, war on poverty, and other liberal democratic federal dispensations. It must be free too of the mistaken liberal conviction that integration, particularly integration of the public schools, is the key to African-American freedom and empowerment. Cruse prescribes that in the 1990s we African-Americans should develop a "politics of black ethnicity" (PBE p. 356). It will address the problem of economic powerlessness through, among other things, the agency of an "independent black political party" and other self-organizational efforts that will contribute to "a total political, economic, cultural, educational, and institutional reorganization of black life" (PBE p. 378). In the absence of such specifically African-American efforts during the 1990s, Cruse predicts that our survival as a people will be in serious jeopardy by the year 2000 (PBE pp. 378, 382).

For our purposes it is important to observe that this social ethical prescription is largely consistent with the political philosophy of black power as outlined by Carmichael and Hamilton in *Black Power: The Politics of Liberation in America*. Like Carmichael and Hamilton, Cruse sees the need for a distinctively African-American platform that includes economic empowerment. He views the development of an independent black political party as "the initial step" and as the instrumental precondition for other contributions to freedom and empowerment—including contributions to coalition efforts (PBE p. 378). Like Carmichael and Hamilton's philosophy of black power, Cruse prefers a "politics of black ethnicity" inclusive of black economic empowerment over an exclusive emphasis upon the politics of civil rights via integration and assimilation.

Cruse offers his philosophy of "plural but equal" as an alternative to the failed policies of integration and assimilation, and as a "racially democratic alternative" to the bad-faith southern white philosophy of "separate-but-equal" (PBE pp. 369–70). Cruse recognizes that African-Americans in the U.S.A. are not wholly separate and not wholly integrated/assimilated. To be sure, despite the integrationist emphasis of traditional civil rights leaders, African-Americans in general, and African-American churches in particular, have seldom desired to be wholly assimilated into the great white American melting pot. On the whole, we do not desire racial integration/assimilation in our family life, nor in our religious life. Most of us prefer racially distinct families, and racially distinct churches and denominations. Rather than racial integration of family and church, we desire equal empowerment within the continuing reality of an ethnically plural society. Accordingly, Cruse's affirmation of ethnic plurality and equality is consistent with the philosophy of black power, and with the philosophy and practice of the independent black church tradition.

While Cruse does not label his work as a philosophy of black power, he does say that what black power "really meant was pluralism" (PBE p. 252). Accordingly, it is appropriate to describe Cruse's philosophy of "plural but equal" as a philosophy of black power.[12] I recognize Cruse's "plural but equal" philosophy as a black power philosophy that, under another name, stresses the need for black political and economic empowerment. Here a philosophy of black power, under the label of "plural but equal," is prescribing the development of a new-style black leadership, a leadership whose politics of black ethnicity includes the development of independent black political parties and institutions pursuing black economic empowerment. According to the philosophy of plural but equal, power to the people includes economic power to the people.[13]

Cruse's historical account of the African-American circumstance and his "plural but equal" philosophy, then, improves upon the political philosophy of black power by more strongly emphasizing the economic empowerment that should be pursued by a politics of black ethnicity. Cruse says that for a politics of black ethnicity, the bottom line should read "economic justice" (PBE p. 385). Furthermore, Cruse's analysis is consistent with that of the Hares, Aborampah, and others who are very much attentive to the increasing deterioration of black family life in the U.S.A. in that they all agree that the continuing heritage of economic powerlessness is at the root of many of our most pressing difficulties.

According to the witness of our music in the 1980s, among the chains that bind us most severely are unstable and difficult male-female-family relations. The witness of the people is that freedom must include such socio-economic empowerment as makes possible better male-female-family relations. The African-American social analysts from the 1980s who are concerned with exercising the power of black people to improve black male-female-family relations acknowledge the need for African-American contributions to coalition efforts to generate national economic and social policies that will bring an end to economic powerlessness. On occasion they acknowledge the need for some considerable exercise of black power to remedy black economic powerlessness. But most of all, they are concerned to prescribe that we African-Americans should educate ourselves about the social and economic forces that conspire to separate black males from black females and black families, so that we might move to heal the schisms that have grown between us and create improved opportunities for the future of black male-female-family-tribal relations.

In the next chapter We shall evaluate these social ethical views of the African-American circumstance, and of the black power that needs to be exercised during the 1990s and beyond, from the churchly perspective of black theology. We shall consider answers to the social ethical question that black theology calls us to consider—What should our African-American religious congregations do during the 1990s and beyond in order to contribute to the comprehensive empowerment of all the people?

NOTES

1. Please see: Robert L. Douglas, "From Blues to Protest/Assertiveness: The Art of Romare Bearden and John Coltrane," *The International Review of African American Art*, vol. 8, no. 2 (1988). Here Douglas says that "one may think of the Blues as a secular counterpart to the Spiritual," and that the "direct contemporary descendant of the Spiritual in the religious realm is Gospel," and that "both Gospel and Blues are musical expressions which often reflect or signify the social conditions of African-American people" (p. 28). In this essay Douglas's thesis is that "there are both Blues and protest elements in John W. Coltrane's music, and there are both Blues and protest elements in Romare Bearden's art" (p. 28).

2. James H. Cone, in his development of black liberation theology, draws upon traditional African-American sources such as music, prayer, and sermons in *The Spirituals and The Blues* (New York: Seabury Press, 1972) and in *God of the Oppressed* (New York: Seabury Press, 1975).

3. The Black Entertainment Television cable broadcast to the Dallas-Ft. Worth metroplex on Monday, November 5, 1990, included these ten consecutive music video shows: (1) a number by Al B Sure; (2) "Just Can't Handle It" by High Five; (3) "Hai Love" by Kwame; (4) George Clinton's "Mothership Connection" as performed by Stanley Clark and George Duke; (5) "So You Like What You See" by Samuelle; (6) "Warning" by Adeva; (7) "Black Cat" by Janet Jackson; (8) "You Haven't Lived" by Witness; (9) "A Thing Called Love" by The Boys; (10) "I Thought It Was Me" by Bell Biv DeVoe. (The last two numbers were from Donnie Simpson's "Video Soul" and the previous eight were from the preceding program and hosted by a person whose name I failed to record.) By my measure, only two of the ten have words that fail to explicate or imply an irreligious conception of love as recreational sex/love-life: "Mothership Connection" and "You Haven't Lived." Of these two, attention to the hip-swinging dance in the video classifies "Mothership Connection" with the other eight in suggesting recreational sex. Thus only one song—"You Haven't Lived"—speaks explicitly of a religious conception of love. The words include something very near to "You haven't lived until you've loved somebody with the love of Jesus."

4. From Stewart's endnotes, see Donald Byrd, "Music Without Aesthetics: How Some Non-Musical Forces and Institutions Influence Change in Black Music," *The Black Scholar* (July-August 1978); Frank Kofsky, *Black Nationalism and the Revolution in Music* (New York, 1970); April Reilly, "The Impact of Technology on Rhythm 'n' Blues," *The Black Perspective in Music*, vol. 1 (1973). For a narrative account of how African-American music has suffered due to Anglo-American influence during the past fifty years, see Nelson George, *The Death of Rhythm and Blues* (New York: Pantheon Books, 1988). For a more general account of how African-

American art (including literature, music, poetry, drama, etc.) has suffered due to Anglo-American control and exploitation made possible by Anglo-American ownership of mass media and property, see Harold Cruse's "Mass Media and Cultural Democracy" in his book *The Crisis of the Negro Intellectual* (New York: William Morrow, 1967).

5. Other literature from the 1980s that emphasizes the relative scarcity of socio-economically advantaged black men in the U.S.A. includes: Gary, L. E., ed., *Black Men*; Gibbs, Jewelle Taylor, ed., *Young, Black, and Male in America: An Endangered Species*; Hare, Nathan and Julia, "The Making of the Black Male Shortage and Its Impact on the Black Family"; Madhubuti, Haki R., "Black Men: Obsolete, Single and Dangerous"; idem, "Were Corners Made for Black Men to Stand On?"; Parham, Thomas A., and Roderick J. McDavis, "Black Men, An Endangered Species: Who's Really Pulling the Trigger?"; Poussaint, Alvin F., "Black Men Must Organize" (an interview); Scott, Joseph W., and James B. Steward, "The Institutional Decimation of the Black American Male"; Staples, Robert, "Black Male Genocide: A Final Solution to the Race Problem in America"; idem, *Black Masculinity: The Black Male's Role in American Society*. And, from the 1970s, remember Jacquelyn Jackson, "But Where Are the Men?" and Samuel Yette, *The Choice: The Issue of Black Survival in America*. From popular literature, see Robert W. Goldfarb, "Black Men Are Last," *New York Times* (March 14, 1980); W. Leavy, "Is the Black Male an Endangered Species?," *Ebony* (August 1983); "A New Generation of Native Sons," *Time* (December 1, 1986), pp. 34–35; Sylvester Monroe, "Brothers," in *Newsweek* (March 23, 1987), p. 55; and William Strickland, "Black Men in Crisis," *Essence* (November 1989). Also see the "special issue" of *Ebony* magazine (August 1986) entitled "The Crisis of the Black Family." This is a very fine treatment of the circumstance of African-American families. It includes attention to the scarcity of marriageable black men, to male-female schism, to economic disadvantage, and to other important matters such as religion and education. Furthermore, this issue prescribes as "the cure" the following: "cure long-standing problems of poverty by ending unemployment, race bias" (p. 144); "stop massive abuse of illegal drugs" (p. 149); "end tensions between black men and women" (p. 153); "make black love and the extended family concept priorities" (p. 158); and "return to the spiritual traditions of black churches and schools" (p. 160).

6. While the Hares agree with the basic liberal conviction that public/governmental and other sectors of society should contribute to improved socio-economic well-being, still the Hares disagree with Wilson's "hidden agenda" approach. Where Wilson seeks to benefit the truly disadvantaged through policies that are universally beneficial, the Hares believe that such universal approaches are too costly (CBSP p. 8). Also, the Hares lament the fact that while on the one hand, and positively, Wilson and Edelman perceive that the so-called explosion in black out-of-wedlock teenage pregnancy is more about decreasing marriage rates than increasing birthrates (because the birthrate among black teenagers has actually been declining for the past twenty years); on the other hand, and negatively, Wilson and Edelman are, nonetheless, more interested in policies designed to cut the pregnancy rate than in policies for increasing the marriage rate (CBSP pp. 8–9).

7. Jawanza Kunjufu's publications include: *Countering the Conspiracy to Destroy Black Boys*; *Countering the Conspiracy to Destroy Black Boys, Volume 2*; *Developing Positive Self-Images and Discipline in Black Children*; *Motivating and Preparing Black Youth to Work*; *To Be Popular or Smart: The Black Peer Group*.

8. The contributors to *Crisis in Black Sexual Politics* are: Bamidele Ade Agbasegbe, Na'im Akbar, Joanna Bower, David R. Burgest, Bebe Moore Campbell, John Hawke Clarke, Harold Cruse, Julia Hare, Nathan Hare, Jacqueline Johnson Jackson, Morris F.X. Jeff, Maulana Karenga, Jawanze Kunjufu, Haki Madhubuti, Joseph Scott, Robert Staples, James Stewart, Alex Swan, and Erica Tollett. There is a foreword by Congressman Gus Savage.

9. On this point, Aborampah references Robert Staples, *The World of Black Singles: Changing Patterns of Male/Female Relations*, and idem, "Race and Marital Status: An Overview." For further reflection upon the tendency for young upwardly mobile-educated-professional blacks ("buppies") to be victim of socialization that contributes to gender conflict, see Nathan and Julia Hare, "The Successful Black Woman's Man Problem," *The Endangered Black Family*. Another reflection upon the successful black woman's man problem is Bebe Moore Campbell, "To Be Black, Gifted, and Alone." Additionally, in his "The Black Male/Female Impasse," Harold Cruse comes to "the inescapable conclusion that the more "successful" we become, the more "status" we achieve, the more "equality" we achieve, the more affluence we gain, the more unworkable do our concepts of marriage and personal relationships on the sexual level become" (CBSP p. 64). A very important and highly controversial work from outside the field of academic sociological scholarship which focuses attention upon the black woman and her socialization as a factor contributing to male-female conflict is Shahrazad Ali, *The Blackman's Guide to Understanding the Blackwoman*. Ali asserts that a large part of the problem with black male-female relations is the black woman's "confusion about her role and purpose" and her "emotional insecurity and related fears" (p. viii). Ali argues that the black woman is "out of control due to her rebellion against the authority of the Blackman." Ali offers her a guide to understanding the black woman in order that the black man will not continue to "stumble around blindly trying to overcome obstacles in a Blackwoman he knows little, if anything, about" (p. ix). The reader may care to consult a rebuttal to Ali's book—Haki R. Madhubuti, ed., *Confusion by Any Other Name: Essays Exploring the Negative Impact of The Blackman's Guide to Understanding the Blackwoman* (Chicago: Third World Press, 1990). The contributors to this collection of essays are: Cynthia Blair, Vivian Gordon, Beverly Guy-Sheftall, Bakari Kitwana, Morris Jeff, Haki Madhubuti, Christine Minor, and Lois Smith Owens.

10. See also Clifton H. Johnson, "A Legacy of La Amistad: Some Twentieth-Century Black Leaders." In this essay Johnson describes the 1839 revolt of 53 Africans aboard the ship *Amistad* as contributing to the formation of the American Missionary Association. It in turn contributed to the development of schools and colleges that produced such outstanding black leaders as Booker T. Washington, W. E. B. DuBois, James Weldon Johnson, William Pickens, Walter White, and Benjamin Hooks. For our purposes it is important to note that Johnson's account of DuBois's break with the NAACP is similar to Cruse's account. Johnson notes that at times "DuBois was the only Black staff member of the organization" (p. 14), and that "when DuBois broke with the NAACP he was accused of deserting Black Americans in their struggle for integration and first-class citizenship by advocating self-segregation. He never, however, advocated that Blacks should accept anything less than equality.... He thought they could have these while also enjoying the solidarity of cultural and economic nationalism. Race pride and cultural nationalism were central themes in his philosophy" (p. 16). Johnson's account is consistent

with the view that it was a philosophy of noneconomic liberalism focused on integration without recourse to economic development and other goals that caused DuBois to break with the NAACP. Johnson goes on to describe DuBois as "the oracle of the Black Power Movement" on account of his cultural nationalism and attention to Africa (p. 17). This is consistent with Cruse's view of DuBois's thought moving away from the NAACP noneconomic liberal integrationist agenda to a more Garveylike regard for a politics and economics of black and African ethnicity. Similarly, Theodore G. Vincent (*Black Power and the Garvey Movement*) pictures DuBois as more in accord with Garvey than is generally recognized. Vincent says, "the errors of the Garveyites during their heyday in the 1920s were well documented and widely publicized by a host of black militants, including Dr. W. E. B. DuBois. In later years, as the relevance of the Garvey approach became more apparent, many of Garvey's one-time enemies, including Dr. DuBois, adopted a more favorable stance toward Garveyism. But nonetheless the early criticisms have retained a dominant position in the historical appraisal of Garveyism" (p. 10). Vincent's text presents "a more balanced picture" (p. 10). Also see Amy Jacques Garvey, *Garvey and Garveyism*.

11. Cruse notes that African-American leadership was identified as being in crisis as early as 1920 in *Crisis* magazine. The article Cruse speaks of is Harry H. Jones's "The Crisis in Negro Leadership." More recently, Malcolm X identified a crisis in African-American leadership. In *The Autobiography of Malcolm X*, Brother Malcolm said: "The American black 'leader's' most critical problem is lack of imagination! His thinking, his strategies, if any, are always limited, at least basically, to only that which is either advised, or approved by the white man" (AMX p. 347). Similarly, Cornel West, in *Prophetic Fragments*, identifies a leadership crisis among black liberals, and the crisis is said to consist in "the inability to forward visions, analyses, and programs that can ameliorate the plight of the black working poor and underclass" (PF p. 59). Also see Louis Farrakhan, "A Crisis in Black Leadership," and Maulana Karenga, "The Crisis of Black Middle Class Leadership: A Critical Analysis."

12. While here I am describing Cruse's "plural but equal" philosophy as circumscribed by the philosophy of black power, some of us may recall that Cruse wrote an unfavorable review of black power in the postscript of his 1967 text, *The Crisis of the Negro Intellectual*. In a postscript entitled "Postscript on Black Power—The Dialogue between Shadow and Substance," Cruse said "the Black Power dialogue does not close the conceptual gap between shadow and substance" (CNI p. 545). So it might seem that I am doing violence to Cruse's work in describing it as a philosophy of black power; however, this is not the case. Let us keep in mind that this postscript was written without benefit of the resources that were subsequently available through the published articulation of the denotative meaning of black power by King, Carmichael-Hamilton, and McKissick. Cruse's postscript was a response to the confused mixture of denotative and connotative meanings that held sway in the popular depictions of 1966 and 1967. Cruse made precisely this point when he wrote "the exact concept of Black Power has not yet been clearly defined. At this writing, as a concept it remains as vague as the former abstractions—Justice and Liberation" (CNI p. 544). Now, thanks to King, to Carmichael-Hamilton, to McKissick, and to others, the transformation of "black power" from confusing, vague, and inflammatory slogan into a clearly denotative philosophy would allow Cruse to say in his 1987 text that what black power really meant was "plural but

equal" (PBE p. 252). Accordingly, it is not wrong to describe "plural but equal" as a more recent version of the philosophy of black power.

13. Cornel West, in *Prophetic Fragments*, teaches us that economic power is not adequately measured by the Weberian index—high income. Rather, justly distributed economic power includes the "ideal of blacks' empowerment over and democratic participation in crucial economic decisions" (p. 52). This is consistent with the philosophy of black power. For instance, Carmichael and Hamilton say: "Our basic premise is that money and jobs are not the final answer to the black man's problems ... the basic goal is not 'welfare colonialism,' as some have called the anti-poverty and other federal programs, but the inclusion of black people at all levels of decision-making. We do not seek to be mere recipients from the decision-making process but participants in it" (BP p. 183).

BIBLIOGRAPHY

Aborampah, Osei-Mensah. "Black Male-Female Relationships: Some Observations" *The Journal of Black Studies*, vol. 19, no. 3 (March 1989).
Aldridge, Delores P. "The Black Family: Socialization and Conflict." *The Western Journal of Black Studies*, vol. 8, no. 4 (1984).
Ali, Shahrazad. *The Blackman's Guide to Understanding the Blackwoman*. Philadelphia: Civilized Publications, 1989.
Campbell, Bebe Moore. "To Be Black, Gifted, and Alone." *Crisis in Black Sexual Politics*, Nathan and Julia Hare, eds. San Francisco: Black Think Tank, 1989.
Carmichael, Stokely and Charles V. Hamilton. *Black Power: The Politics of Liberation in America*. New York: Vintage Books, 1967.
Cone, James H. *God of the Oppressed*. New York: Seabury Press, 1975.
——. *The Spirituals and the Blues*. New York: Seabury Press, 1972.
——. "What is the Church?" *Speaking the Truth: Ecumenism, Liberation, and Black Theology*. Grand Rapids: William B. Eerdmans, 1986.
Cruse, Harold. "The Black Male/Female Impasse." *Crisis in Black Sexual Politics*, Nathan and Julia Hare, eds. San Francisco: Black Think Tank, 1989.
——. *The Crisis of the Negro Intellectual*. New York: William Morrow, 1967, 1984.
——. "Mass Media and Cultural Democracy." *The Crisis of the Negro Intellectual*. New York: William Morrow, 1967, 1984.
——. *Plural But Equal: Blacks and Minorities in America's Plural Society*. New York: William Morrow, 1987.
Dewart, Janet, ed. *The State of Black America 1989*. New York: National Urban League, 1989.
Douglas, Robert L. "From Blues to Protest/Assertiveness: The Art of Romare Bearden and John Coltrane." *The International Review of African American Art*, vol. 8, no. 2 (1988).
Edelman, Marian Wright. "An Agenda for Empowerment." *Essence* (May 1988).
Farrakhan, Louis. "A Crisis in Black Leadership." *Essence* (June 1984).
Garvey, Amy Jacques. *Garvey and Garveyism*. Jamaica: United Printers Ltd., 1961.
Gary, L.E., ed. *Black Men*. Beverly Hills: Sage Publications, 1981.
George, Nelson. *The Death of Rhythm and Blues*. New York: Pantheon Books, 1988.
Gibbs, Jewelle Taylor, ed. *Young, Black, and Male in America: An Endangered Species*. Dover, Mass.: Auburn House, 1988.

Harding, Vincent. *There is a River: The Black Struggle for Freedom in America*. New York: Harcourt Brace Jovanovich, 1981.

Hare, Nathan. "Revolution Without a Revolution: The Psychology of Sex and Race." *The Black Scholar*, vol. 13, numbers 4, 5 (Summer 1982).

Hare, Nathan and Julia. *Bringing the Black Boy to Manhood: The Passage*. San Francisco: Black Think Tank, 1985.

Hare, Nathan and Julia. *The Broken Patriarchy: Bringing the Black Girl to Womanhood: The Passage*. San Francisco: Black Think Tank (publication pending).

Hare, Nathan and Julia. *The Endangered Black Family: Coping With the Unisexualization and Coming Extinction of the Black Race*. San Francisco: Black Think Tank, 1986, 1984.

Hare, Nathan and Julia. "The Making of the Black Male Shortage and Its Impact on the Black Family." *Crisis in Black Sexual Politics*. San Francisco: Black Think Tank, 1989.

Hare, Nathan and Julia. "The Successful Black Woman's Man Problem." *The Endangered Black Family*. San Francisco: Black Think Tank, 1984, 1986.

Hare, Nathan and Julia, eds. *Crisis in Black Sexual Politics*. San Francisco: Black Think Tank, 1989.

Jackson, Jacquelyn. "But Where Are the Men?" *The Black Scholar* (December 1971).

Johnson, Clifton H. "A Legacy of La Amistad: Some Twentieth-Century Black Leaders." *The International Review of African American Art*, vol. 8, no. 2 (1988).

Jones, Harry H. "The Crisis in Negro Leadership." *Crisis*, vol. 19, no. 5 (March 1920).

Karenga, Maulana. "The Crisis of Black Middle Class Leadership: A Critical Analysis." *The Black Scholar*, vol. 13, no. 6 (Fall 1982).

Kunjufu, Jawanza. *Countering the Conspiracy to Destroy Black Boys*. Chicago: African American Images, 1983.

———. *Countering the Conspiracy to Destroy Black Boys, Vol. II*. Chicago: African American Images, 1986.

———. *Developing Positive Self-Images and Discipline in Black Children*. Chicago: African-American Images, 1984.

———. *Motivating and Preparing Black Youth to Work*. Chicago: African American Images, 1986.

———. *To Be Popular or Smart: The Black Peer Group*. Chicago: African American Images, 1988.

Madhubuti, Haki. "Black Men: Obsolete, Single and Dangerous." *Crisis in Black Sexual Politics*, Nathan and Julia Hare, eds. San Francisco: Black Think Tank, 1989.

———. "Were Corners Made for Black Men to Stand On?" *The Black Scholar*, vol. 18, no. 3 (May/June 1987).

Parham, Thomas A., and Roderick J. McDavis. "Black Men, An Endangered Species: Who's Really Pulling the Trigger?" *The Journal of Counseling and Development*, vol. 66 (September 1987).

Poussaint, Alvin F. "Black Men Must Organize." *The Black Scholar*, vol. 18, no. 3 (May/June 1987).

Roberts, J. Deotis. *Roots of a Black Future: Family and Church*. Philadelphia: Westminster Press, 1980.

Scott, Joseph W., and James B. Steward. "The Institutional Decimation of the Black

American Male." *The Western Journal of Black Studies*, vol. 2 (Summer 1978).

Staples, Robert. "Black Male Genocide: A Final Solution to the Race Problem in America." *The Black Scholar*, vol. 18, no. 3 (May/June, 1987).

——. *Black Masculinity: The Black Male's Role in American Society*. San Francisco: The Black Scholars Press, 1982.

——. "Race and Marital Status: An Overview." *Black Families*, H. P. McAdoo, ed. Beverly Hills: Sage Publications, 1981.

——. *The World of Black Singles: Changing Patterns of Male/Female Relations*. Westport, Conn.: Greenwood Press, 1981.

Stewart, James B. "Relationships between Black Males and Females in Rhythm and Blues Music of the 1960s and 1970s." *The Western Journal of Black Studies*, vol. 3, no. 3 (Fall 1979).

Vincent, Theodore G. *Black Power and the Garvey Movement*. Berkeley: Ramparts Press, 1971.

West, Cornel. *Prophetic Fragments*. Grand Rapids: Eerdmans/ Trenton, N.J.: Africa World Press, 1988.

Wilson, William Julius. *The Truly Disadvantaged: The Inner City, the Underclass, and Public Policy*. Chicago: University of Chicago Press, 1987.

X, Malcolm. *The Autobiography of Malcolm X*, Alex Haley, ed. New York: Ballantine Books, 1964, 1973.

Yette, Samuel. *The Choice: The Issue of Black Survival in America*. New York: Putnam, 1971.

CHAPTER SIX

Servant of the People

Analyzing Black Power Agenda from the Churchly Perspective of Black Theology

Our understanding of the witness of Scripture is that we ought to break bread together (bread being understood as a symbol for the various resources that nourish wholesome social existence), and moreover we understand from the biblical witness that this is the absolutely essential aspect of right relation to God—indeed, it is the ethic of breaking bread that in God's final judgment separates righteousness from unrighteousness. The witness of our music, this time the witness of our churchly music, is that there is a necessary connection between right relation to God and bread breaking or righteous relation to others. When we sing "let us break bread together on our knees," as we do during holy communion services, we witness to a fundamental connection between the practice of breaking bread and prayful God-consciousness.

This black God-conscious social ethical prescription—that we break bread together—is understood to apply to every social circumstance. It is at this point that black theological social ethics can offer a prescriptive word to the whole world. Our prayerfully prescriptive witness is that, regardless of social circumstance or location, God requires that we break bread together. It is important for us to offer this social ethical word to the world, but on this occasion, in this book, we have more local work to do. While the ethic of breaking bread calls black theological social ethics to affirm the bread-breaking aspects of liberal and radical and other secular social ethical thought, and while the ethic of breaking bread calls us to encourage and support genuinely bread-breaking coalition efforts globally, nonetheless, black theological social ethical reflection must also be responsible for addressing more local questions about the righteous exercise of black power.

Nathan and Julia Hare, Jawanza Kunjufu, Osei-Mensah Aborampah, and many other African-American scholars in the U.S.A. are raising and answering the question of black empowerment in terms of black people's responsibility to address the difficulties in our intimate family and tribal relationships. For example, when Na'im Akbar, former president of the National Association of Black Psychologists, speaks of black power, he speaks first of the black family.[1] These social ethical reflections are distinguished from liberal social ethical reflections by the greater concern with what we black folk can do ourselves to advance the struggle for comprehensive socio-economic empowerment.

The philosophy of black power circumscribes social ethical reflection upon, as brother Ture (Carmichael) puts it, "black folk taking care of black folk's business." It is on account of their emphasis upon black folk taking better care of black family and tribal relations that we may describe the social ethical reflections of the Hares, Kunjufu, Aborampah, Akbar, and others under the category of black power. Also, Harold Cruse's focus upon African-American leadership, and the need for an independent black political party concerned with the economic empowerment of African-Americans is obviously within the sphere of black power's social ethical reflections.

From the churchly perspective of black theology, perhaps the most significant oversight characterizing much of the social ethical reflection upon the exercise of black power pertains to the typical failure of social scientists to explicate or appreciate the extent to which their questions are religious questions. Correspondingly, there is their failure to appreciate the fact that our churches and religious communities are indispensable resources for black empowerment. The question of the exercise of black power in the U.S.A. is a question that cannot reasonably fail to include questions about exercising the power of black churches and other black religious communities. Nowhere in the black community of the U.S.A. can one find more bread, more money, more talent, and more resources under the full discretionary control of black people than in our churches and other religious communities. Where else can one go in the heart of the most impoverished ghetto and find committees of black women and men regularly, and legally, administering budgets of hundreds of thousands and millions of dollars? In what sphere of life save for religion have black people in mass claimed for themselves independently empowered and self-directed institutions? Where is black power in the U.S.A. if not in our churches? Reflection upon the power of black churches and black religion is a necessary aspect of any adequate social ethic that prescribes the exercise of black power.

RELIGIOUS RITUAL: LET THE PEOPLE DANCE

In their social ethical reflections, the philosophers of black power are largely negligent of religious matters, but they are not totally negligent of religion. They are most aware of religion at the point where they prescribe the development of rites of passage. Aborampah, for instance, in his call for black people to institutionalize transitional rites of passage as a socialization technique by which to enable black children to avoid a future characterized by schismatic gender conflict, is conscious of the spiritual and religious aspects of his recommendation. Though he offers hardly more than two paragraphs concerning religion, what he says is significant. He regrets "the fact that socialization of many black children today is largely devoid of any meaningful spiritual content" (BMFR p. 336). Drawing upon the example of traditional African religious ritual, Aborampah calls upon black churches and other major black organizations to develop socialization techniques including ceremonial rituals, particularly rites of passage, that provide the spiritual content essential to "value revival."

Nearly any reasonable call for the exercise of black power in the U.S.A. needs to include black churches and religious communities. Moreover, when black people are called upon to take better care of the business of intimate family and tribal relations—and most especially when that call includes a request for value reviving and religiously informed ritual—this is a social ethical imperative that is precisely and uniquely appropriate to black churches and religious communities. And indeed it is the case that some black churches are already responding to this imperative by developing rites of passage and other socializing programs. It is my hope that increasing numbers of church leaders, educators, artists, and others will contribute to such efforts. It is surely the case that we need to employ religious ritual and other socializing resources to provide present and coming generations with more righteous values and habits of thought and deed.

Our effort to be fully attentive to indigenous African-American and traditional African resources requires that I speak again about a resource that the literature of socio-scientific reflection has largely ignored. I speak again of our music and of our tradition of dance.

Let us return to the place of my father's house, to Greensboro, North Carolina. In 1960 four African-American students from North Carolina Agricultural and Technical State University staged a sit-in at Woolworth's Cafeteria. This was a most audacious act, which for many of us signaled the beginning of a widespread social movement against de jure segregation in the southern states.[2] It was in Greensboro, on east Market Street, not far from A&T State University, that I learned to appreciate a rather obvious and, as I shall argue, highly significant feature of the present African-American circumstance. On a hot summer's night of 1986, I was bicycling on Market Street and came upon a popular night club or disco where young African-Americans gather for dancing. As I approached the club I could hear and feel the thump of the bass and the accelerated beat of foot-stomping music. On the other side of the street, almost opposite the front of the disco, there was an African-American evangelist preaching quite eloquently from the back of a van. On one side of the street, there was the rhythm, the bass, and the beat. On the other side of the street, there was preaching and the gospel. As I, along with many others, passed down Market Street, we felt the alternate and seemingly opposite attractions of dance on one side and of religion on the other. This experience is typical of the African-American circumstance in the U.S.A. On Market Street in Greensboro, North Carolina, as almost everywhere else in these United States, African-Americans must choose or alternate between dance and religion, because dance floors and religion exist always on opposite and contrary sides of the street.

The idea that the drums, the rhythm, the bass, the beat and dancing are strictly nonreligious or secular, and always to be identified with the unrighteous and irreligious side of the street, is an idea that was imposed upon black African peoples by white Euro-American oppressors. During slavery, they took as much of our freedom as they could harness. They took our drums. They placed shackles on our feet. And they told us not to dance. They said dancing was sinful. And we believed them. And so our drums, our rhythm and beat and dancing—these traditional African modalities—are given over to the irreligious side of the street.[3] How very European and non-African of us.

For traditional and ancient African peoples, dancing was a normal part of religious worship (for example, in Scripture, 2 Samuel 6:14, we are told that "David danced before the Lord with all his might"). There is no reason, except for the prejudice and inhibitions of those who do not dance, that religion should relegate drums, basses, rhythm, and dancing to the unrighteous side of the street. The exile of these instruments and resources was a white racist and deliberately oppressive act. The continued exile of dance from our religious life is a mightily debilitating habit.

It is very unfortunate that on the whole we religious African-Americans have not yet emancipated ourselves from the Euro-American view that religion must always keep our dancing on the far side of the street. This is unfortunate because, as one can see from the flow of our people on Market Street and elsewhere, there are large numbers of our young people who cannot be reached in words that have no rhythm, no bass, and no beat. Many of our young people are telling us: "If it aint got no bass, if it aint got no beat, if it don't make me wanna stamp my feet, it aint gonna reach this side of the street." And it may be that we need to listen more closely to this message in our more general efforts to better socialize and educate our young ones. It may be that teachers who do not dance are suffering a significant pedagogical deficiency. And it may be that musicians and dancers who do not educate and teach righteousness are being irresponsible to the needs of our young ones. Maybe M.C. Hammer, Queen Latifah, Too Short, and James Brown need to be employed as teachers for those who are unreached without rap and rhythm and beat. When the rhythms that are part of the black African soul seek the physical and spiritual and social release of dancing, because there is no dancing among Europeanized religious congregations, those who must dance are called away from religion, and to the unrighteous side of the street.

Let the people dance. Empower them with opportunity to dance to the glory of God, rather than to the perennial themes of unrighteousness. We must do something about the music, and something about dancing. We must sing songs that are good enough to sing. We must bring the drums, and the bass, the foot-stomping rhythm, the dance floor, and the experience of dance back into our religious life. Dance can empower. Dance can teach. Dance can heal. Dance can celebrate and glorify. But if the only dancing there is is hinged upon the culture of unrighteousness, then the basic black and African and human and divine urge to dance is transformed into a force for unrighteousness. And then the urge to dance becomes an invitation to a killing field. The dance floor and its unholy perimeter becomes the locus for illicit and recreational sex, for the exchange of alcohol, tobacco, and other drugs, as well as the staging ground for violent confrontations. If such unholy dance floors are the only dance floors, then the urge to dance that is good—and righteous and spiritual and uplifting and black and African and human and divine—is transformed into a compulsion to mingle amid the culture of unrighteousness.

If our efforts to develop value-reviving and religiously informed rituals are at all guided by traditional African examples, as Aborampah suggests, and if, as Aborampah requires, such rituals and rites are to be suitable and appropriate to the current generation of African-Americans (BMFR p. 339), then a religious appropriation of dance is clearly called for. We need to recover the religious and righteous socializing power of dance. For those of us who are black and African and who have soul and rhythm, there needs to be a dance floor on the religious side of the street.[4]

SOCIALIZATION AND EDUCATION

Those African-American social analysts who in the 1980s undertook to answer the question that the philosophy of black power calls us to answer were concerned with the exercise of the black community's own socializing power to address problems of family and tribal relations. We are advised of an urgent need to heal male-female schism, to reclaim the positive aspects of black patriarchy, and of the need for more righteous socialization of black youth, and of black males in particular. Moreover, we are advised that our socialization techniques should include religious rituals and, in particular, rites of passage. Now further reflection has indicated that these rituals and rites should not exclude music and dance.

Another approach to the exercise of black power to improve the circumstance of black families and tribes is present in the example of the black church women's movement of the late nineteenth and early twentieth centuries. During these decades the black women of the major African-American churches and denominations in the U.S.A. organized their own gender-specific conventions.

The black church women's movement, according to Evelyn Brooks, was equally committed to the struggle against socio-economic-political structures of inequality, and to a "moralistic emphasis" upon personal values and conduct. In her article—"Religion, Politics, and Gender: The Leadership of Nannie Helen Burroughs"—Brooks points to the example of Nannie Helen Burroughs, leader of the black Baptist Women's Convention from 1900 to 1961, the year of her death. Burroughs's attempt to answer the characteristic question of black power and black theology in a speech on the topic, "What Must the Negro Do to Be Saved?," is summarized by Brooks as a call for first, "a God-centered life," second, a race-focused message of uplift, and third, in Burroughs's own words, "a glorified womanhood" (RPG p. 21). From Brooks we learn that the glorified womanhood called for by Burroughs and others in the black church women's movement is characterized by a commitment to women's suffrage/rights and other liberating political policies, and by a strong emphasis upon the black woman's and the black church's contributions to the socialization and education of black people.

Toinette M. Eugene's article—"Moral Values and Black Womanists" teaches us that the black women's movement of the late nineteenth and early twentieth centuries, along with contemporary black womanist thought, differs from white feminist movements in that, for black women, "domesticity has never been seen as entirely oppressive but rather as a vehicle for building family life" (MVBW p. 26). Eugene describes the difference between white women's models for theology and black women's models in terms of the white feminist conception of liberation as mutuality and equality, in contrast to the black women's inclusion of "a theology of servant leadership" based upon such exemplary models as Nannie Helen Burroughs, Charlotte Hawkins Brown, and Mary McLeod Bethune (MVBW pp. 29-30). This then is not "feminist theology," nor is it "black feminist theology"; rather it is "womanist" or "black womanist theology."[5] Black womanist theology finds a model for the Christian moral life in the black church women's movement. The leaders of the black church women's movement were seriously concerned with exercising the socializing power of black churches and institutions to contribute to the empowerment of black families here and abroad, especially in Africa.

Education, including not only formal academic learning but also family values and domestic or home building and home maintenance skills, was among the important socializing powers employed by the black church women's movement. Their religiously motivated concern with education, and with being educators and teachers, is underlined by Eugene when she writes:

> The religious consciousness of the black freedwoman in the latter nineteenth century focused on "uplifting the black community." The

> black female was taught that her education was meant not only to uplift her but also to prepare her for a life of service in the overall community.... This attitude provided an additional impetus for black women, such as Nannie Helen Burroughs, Charlotte Hawkins Brown, and Mary McLeod Bethune, to found schools. Although the curricula of these schools included academic subjects, there were large doses of industrial arts courses, particularly homemaking, and an environment that enforced codes of morality and thrift. [MVBW p. 29]

The religion of the black church women's movement was devoted to the empowerment of the people through the ethic of breaking bread. Education and socialization in the arts and sciences of home economics were an important part of the bread they shared with us.

The moral sentiments of the leaders of the black church women's movement were echoed in Stokely Carmichael's 1972 speech to the members of the Black Student Movement at the University of North Carolina at Chapel Hill, when he taught us that we are morally obliged to use our education for the empowerment of the people. Carmichael reminded us that it was on account of the sacrifice and struggle of others that we were blessed with an opportunity to receive education at the historically and predominantly white University of North Carolina. Those of us who are harvesting the fruit of our parents' and ancestors' struggle are called to share these blessings with others.

Carmichael's call for us to employ our education and other resources to advance the struggle for liberation and empowerment is very much like the message of black empowerment espoused by Nannie Helen Borroughs, Mary McLeod Bethune, and other leaders of the black church women's movement in the late nineteenth and early twentieth centuries. It is true that these women were more likely to have spoken of themselves as "Negro" than as "black," and to have spoken of "uplift" rather than "empowerment." Nonetheless, their moral commitment to the idea that black women, black people, and black churches should exercise their powers of education and socialization in ways that improve the circumstances of black homes, families, and tribes here and abroad places their social ethical thought unequivocally within the category of social ethical thinking we now call the philosophy of black power.

The power of the black church women's movement is evident in the number of schools, academies, and colleges founded, supported, and staffed by black women, and by the black churches and denominations of which they have been the majority membership. The numerous black colleges and schools, and hundreds of secondary and primary schools that were born and nurtured by the efforts of black women and their church and denominational groups, are historical examples of the exercise of black power, of black church power, and black woman power.

What I consider to be very nearly the bottom line in our reflection upon exercising black power to better educate and socialize present and coming generations is the common sense awareness that cultivating the vision and habits of righteousness in thought and deed requires lots of time and attention. It will not suffice to steal one or two hours per week for righteousness sake when a great many more hours of that same week are spent imbibing the sexual and homicidal fantasies of dirty old white men—that is, watching television.[6] It will not suffice to sing four righteous hymns on Sunday morning when long hours of every day, including Sunday, are spent tuned to mass media and music and dance that relentlessly encourage unrighteous thinking. It will not suffice to emphasize black history month, or the birthdays of Martin Luther King, Jr., and Malcolm X, without having also ensured that truthful African-American, traditional African, and ancient African contributions are daily part of classroom, mass media, home, community, and churchly education. If our full time and attention is taken by the culture of unrighteousness, then a few hours of ritualizing can hardly undo such relentlessly cultivated habits of thought and deed.[7] While it is needful that righteous ritual mark the transitions from boyhood and girlhood to manhood and womanhood, righteous rituals need also mark transitions from one day to the next, even from one part of a day to another. Just as every day, all day, all night, the music of unrighteousness in combination with the televised fantasies of money, sex, physical beauty and violence, reach out to claim our attention for the purpose of stimulating and shaping our consumer instincts, we must every day, all day, and all night, aspire to reclaim the time and attention of our young ones. Education and socialization are all day everyday concerns.

Nathan and Julia Hare describe our task in terms of "regaining control of our children's minds" and "simultaneously regaining control of our own" (CBSP p. 32). From a more religious perspective, the dean of the Howard School of Divinity, Lawrence N. Jones, speaks in terms of "transmitting the faith" from one generation to another ("Transmitting the Faith: From Generation to Generation"). Similarly, in her book, *Inheriting Our Mothers' Gardens: Feminist Theology in Third World Perspective*, Katie Geneva Cannon (borrowing from Alice Walker's language in *In Search of Our Mother's Gardens*) speaks in terms of surviving the present blight and cultivating an inheritance from our mothers' gardens.[8]

Since the late nineteenth and early twentieth centuries, African-Americans in the U.S.A. have succeeded in turning much of the responsibility for the education and socialization of black children and black youth over to institutions where white power prevails, and where our mothers' gardens are rarely attended. The many elementary and secondary schools that were the fruit of black woman and black church power in the nineteenth and early twentieth centuries have been all but wholly replaced by allegedly "integrated" public schools. Moreover, far too many of the colleges and universities founded by the exercise of black power have ceased to exist, and many of those remaining are in serious difficulty. The power of black people, of black churches, and of black women and men exercising full responsibility for the nurture, education, and socialization of black children and youth is very much missed at this end of the twentieth century.

In the 1990s, when the call for the exercise of black power to better nurture, educate, and socialize black youth is received by black churches, we recognize that we are being called to recover a power that we have here lately surrendered too easily to the institutions of white power. We are now called to the traditional task of doing what the institutions and structures of white power have failed to do for us. Black theology, drawing upon the traditions of black churches and of the black church women's movement, recognizes that we are now being called to do what is already part of our churchly tradition. Religious ritual, education, day-care, nursery, preschool, church school, Sunday school, summer school, Bible school, primary, elementary, junior high, and high schools, adult education, teacher education, college and university schooling, religious and theological education, medical schools, health care, birth care, death care, counseling, legal aid, financial aid, and more, are all within the traditional repertoire of the black church. The black church women's movement and numerous black religious associations have contributed to the black church's long tradition of responding affirmatively to the call to exercise black power to better nurture, educate, and socialize black youth, and black people generally.[9]

The call to which the black church women's movement responded in 1890 is being heard again as we begin the 1990s. Again, we are called to see to the education and socialization of black children and black people. This social ethical agenda is appropriate to our present circumstance. Indications are that in the 1990s and beyond, black organizations, institutions, and churches will be increasingly called upon to exercise power in the areas of education and socialization.

The present circumstances of African-American children, youth, and families in the U.S.A. demand that we approach the twenty-first century with a collective purpose that includes the socializing agenda that brought us into the twentieth century. In many instances this will mean exercising greater power over and within the public school systems. In many instances we may be called to develop supplemental or alternative educational systems.[10] Here it is not my purpose to consider the precise form that the exercise of black power in the areas of socialization and education should take. Instead, my purpose is simply to acknowledge that our present circumstance calls for the exercise of much greater black power in these areas, and also to recall that the exercise of this kind of black power is entirely consistent with our religious and churchly heritage.

REFLECTION ON FAMILY LIBERATION

Black theological attention to sociological literature describing the circumstance of black families in the U.S.A. in terms of crisis began with J.

Deotis Roberts's *Roots of a Black Future: Family and Church*. At the beginning of the 1980s Roberts started with a theological interest in "the family as a symbol of a deeper understanding of the church" (RBF p. 7). His "main purpose" was "to open up important ecclesiological considerations for black theology" (RBF p. 8). Roberts enabled us to see the black church as the extended family of God; to see the extended black family as a "domestic church" (RBF p. 80); and to see that the past, present, and future of black churches and black families are mutually related (RBF p. 132). Roberts referred us to the sociological work of Moynihan, the Hares, Robert Staples, and others to draw attention to the crisis circumstance of black family life. He taught us "that the black church has as a primary task the strengthening of black families" (RBF p. 132). Roberts, then, was the first black theologian of the 1980s to make "family liberation" a priority item on the black churchly agenda.

Empower the People is built, in large part, upon our acceptance of the truth-value of the theological and ecclesiological point that Roberts develops—that the past, the present, and the future of black families and black churches are positively related. Our attention to sociological studies of African-American family life follows in the direction indicated by Roberts's call for increased attention to matters of family and tribe from our theological and churchly communities (RBF p. 8). And, as is consistent with the Africa-consciousness of the philosophy of black power, Roberts has taught us that our reflections upon black family and church must include attention to African rootage (RBF p. 7).

An earlier churchly response to Roberts's family liberation agenda is Wallace Charles Smith's *The Church in the Life of the Black Family*. Smith (pastor of First Baptist Church in Nashville, Tennessee) identifies his text as a "pastoral theology" and as a "black family theology" that seeks to respond to Roberts's call for black churchly and theological attention to the social circumstances of African-American families (CLBF pp. 13, 74). Smith's theological reflection is based, in part, upon Roberts's vision of the mutuality between the black family and the black church such that one can serve as model for the other and vice versa (CLBF p. 74). Smith's pastoral reflections consist in developing a "family ministry" and a "call to action" that present "the potential for liberation available to blacks through a cooperative effort between churches and families" (CLBF p. 24).

Smith follows in the direction indicated by Roberts also in that he is attentive to traditional African-American and native African resources. For example, Smith is critical of sociological reflections upon the black family because so frequently their conception of family as nuclear family rather than as extended family based upon traditional African-American and native African models does not allow for an appreciation of the strengths and virtues of black family responsiveness to oppressive circumstances (CLBF pp. 34–40, 55, 59–62).

One of the distinctive merits of Smith's analysis is his attention to the status of our elderly. And again, Smith's attention to the well-being of elderly African-Americans is, in part, a function of his appropriation of traditional African thinking about family and tribe. The increasingly at risk well-being of our old ones is an important, but frequently neglected, aspect of African-American family crisis. Accordingly, Smith's call for churchly action on behalf of black families is about the liberation and empowerment of both nuclear and extended families—inclusive of our elderly (CLBF p. 41).[11]

Smith goes beyond Roberts, and beyond *Empower the People*, by offering a collection of educational and curricular suggestions and guides for church and Christian education programs designed to improve African-American self-images, and to make other contributions—including economic empowerment efforts—to the enrichment of African-American family life. Smith prescribes, and offers models for, churchly efforts to develop "a comprehensive approach to family enrichment" (CLBF p. 85). Smith's recommendations include such practical bread-breaking efforts as referral services, home health services, nutrition services, transportation services, communications services, legal services, housing, family enrichment, education counseling, and community improvement projects (CLBF pp. 113–52).

According to the direction indicated by Roberts and Smith, according to our churchly ethic of breaking bread, and in accordance with sociological accounts of the present and projected future circumstance of African-American families, our churchly mission for the 1990s is very clear. Our churchly tasks of Christian education, socialization, counseling, and ministry must include vastly increased investments of time, attention, talent, money, and other resources in black family liberation efforts.[12]

LEADERSHIP AND ECONOMIC EMPOWERMENT

Another aspect of African-American existence that is regularly described in terms of "crisis" is leadership, and like the black family crisis, this one has been with us for more than a generation. As Harold Cruse notes, this crisis was publicized in a 1920 article by Harry H. Jones entitled "The Crisis in Negro Leadership." For Cruse, one of the signal moments in the escalation of this crisis was W.E.B. DuBois' split with the NAACP executive board "during an internal debate over the merits of segregation versus integration" in 1934 (PBE p. 42). Harold Cruse's survey of African-American leadership styles since DuBois indicates that this crisis is still with us.

In *Plural But Equal: A Critical Study of Blacks and Minorities in America's Plural Society*, Harold Cruse describes this crisis in terms of black leadership's traditional, and mistaken, commitment to noneconomic liberalism and integration, especially integration of the public school systems, and in terms of failure to develop independent ethnic agenda and institutions, and to pursue black economic empowerment. Accordingly, Cruse prescribes the emergence of a new leadership style that pursues the development of independent black political parties and institutions and he insists that black social and political institutions pursue black economic empowerment.

Cruse's analysis is not ecclesiologically and theologically reflective, but he is attentive to the presence of African-American church leaders. This is in part because any good survey, especially a cross-generational survey, of African-American leadership styles will find our church and religious leaders generously represented. From sources more attentive to religion, we know that very often African-American church leaders address social issues in civil libertarian language—civil rights, equal rights, voting rights, democracy, representation, equal protection, integration. This runs the risk of being understood as nothing more than the integrationist "noneconomic liberalism" that characterizes the kind of leadership that Cruse objects to. For example, Peter J. Paris studies the official records of the leaders of the African Methodist Episcopal Church and the National Baptist Convention, U.S.A., Inc.—*The Social Teachings of the Black Churches*. He finds these records "replete with evidence showing that the thought and action of the black churches have been guided more by their ideal vision of a racially integrated society than by the idea of racial development" (ST p. 45).

High-level official documents may indicate that African-American church leaders are unequivocally committed to integration. But the origins and history of the black "protestant" churches testify more strongly to a de facto commitment to racially independent empowerment—"plural but equal." Paris makes this point when he contrasts what black church leaders have said in high-level official documents with "what in fact they had become—practitioners of a racial pluralism that shunned both wholesale assimilationism and racial separatism" (ST pp. 78–80). Paris describes the "racial pluralism" of the black churches as an effort to "embody racial assimilation and racial separation in a dynamic and creative equilibrium" (ST p. 80). Furthermore, as we have already seen, the churchly perspective of black theology, including as it does the example and heritage of the independent black church movement and a theologically informed appropriation of the philosophy of black power, affirms a conception of freedom that includes comprehensive social, political, and economic empowerment. Therefore black theological social ethical reflection finds that it is appropriate for the black church to exercise, as it often does, the kind of leadership that Cruse prescribes—a leadership that does not restrict its social ethical concerns to civil rights conceived as noneconomic liberalism and integration.[13]

Peter J. Paris offers another social ethical analysis of African-American religious leadership in the United States in his book *Black Leaders in Conflict: Joseph H. Jackson, Martin Luther King, Jr., Adam Clayton Powell, Jr., Malcolm X*. These four leaders are taken to represent four diverse styles of leadership. Jackson is identified as representative of a priestly style, King as the prophetic style, Powell as political reformer, and Malcolm as political nationalist (BLC pp. 192–95). Like Cruse, Paris recognizes a crisis in African-American leadership. Paris also describes a crisis of conflict and public disagreement and failure to cooperate between these four types of African-American religious leadership (BLC pp. 11–12).

In order to overcome this crisis, and thereby create opportunity for the better exercise of the power of African-American religious leadership, Paris offers a systematic analysis of the social ethical reflections of these four black religious leaders. Paris shows that their conceptions of the African-American circumstance are diverse, yet complementary, and that the implied forms of social action are also diverse, yet complementary (BLC pp. 12–13). Paris feels that an increased awareness of the mutual compatibility of these four understandings of our circumstance, and of the power we might rightly exercise, can provide the ground for improved relationship and coalition efforts between diverse African-American religious leaders and communities. *Black Leaders in Conflict*, says Paris, "lays the foundation for a loosely constructed coalition composed of those who have various understandings of racism and who advocate various forms of action on the basis of those understandings" (BLC p. 13). Paris prescribes cooperative and loosely federated coalition efforts between formerly contentious and conflicting black religious communities based upon increased awareness of the common ground and complementary resources provided by the diverse and mutually compatible views of four black religious leaders.

The Reverend Joseph H. Jackson was president of the National Baptist Convention, U.S.A., Inc., from 1953 to 1982. The formal outlines of Jackson's theological social ethic are described by Paris in terms of the basic principle of the parenthood of God and the kinship of all humanity (citing Jackson's 1971 address to the convention, BLC p. 46). Racial oppression violates this principle. Therefore Christians must be committed to the struggle for freedom, but the methods they employ:

> must be judged in the light of that social order that Jesus called the Kingdom of God ..., and based on the brotherhood of all mankind and the fatherhood of God. ... Every method must be tried and tested by the spirit and ethics of Jesus, and the church must align itself with those procedures that can be sanctioned and validated by the spirit and teachings of Jesus Christ. [from Jackson's 1961 address, BLC p. 47]

This view, which Jackson represents as the faith of farmer-preachers, is consistent with black theological reflection. Jackson agrees with black theology's commitment to freedom, and with black theology's ethical insistence upon judging our existence and mode of struggle by reference to God's kingdom.

Despite this formal agreement between Jackson's theological ethic and the literature of black theology, it is widely known that Jackson rejected the language of black power, and that Jackson explicitly rejected Cone's

Black Theology of Liberation. More than this, Jackson even offered explicit rejection of Ghandi's philosophy, and by clear implication, rejection of King's civil rights efforts (BLC p. 64). Formally the two Baptist preachers and black theology agree that Christian social ethical prescriptions are measured against God's standard of the kingdom/righteousness given in the gospel witness to Jesus. But Jackson's way of measuring social action is different in that it excludes the techniques of civil disobedience. And from here the differences between Jackson's way of measuring social action and that offered by King and by black theological reflection become even more serious.

According to Paris, Jackson rules out civil disobedience because "those who practice civil disobedience are anti-American, enemies of the state" (BLC p. 65). Jackson's judgments about the kingdom are strongly shaped by his unexcelled faith in the goodness of the United States, and by his uniting of Christianity with U.S. patriotism. Jackson's union of "love of country" with "love of Christ" is such a strong union that love of Christ can never issue in civil disobedience, not even in nonviolent civil disobedience (BLC p. 66). Jackson's elevation of U.S. patriotism to the level of religion — a view that Jackson calls "Christian patriotism" — is unique even among his followers in the Baptist convention, and among farmer-preachers as well.

Moreover, as one can learn from Taylor Branch's *Parting the Waters: America in the King Years 1954–63*, there were other real and serious differences between Jackson and King over matters of denominational politics and social ethics. These differences were serious enough to place Jackson and King in opposition to each other in several very intense struggles for control of the National Baptist Convention, U.S.A. Throughout his presidency, Jackson was able to frustrate efforts by King and others to bring the resources of the National Baptist Convention, U.S.A., into the struggle for civil rights.

In regard to the philosophy of black power per se, Paris reports that Jackson understands black power to be "a new form of racism" (BLC p. 67). He "opposes Black Theology on similar grounds" (BLC p. 68). But, on the other hand, Paris reports that "the concept of Black self-development and Black independence is and has been a consistent one throughout Jackson's public life" (BLC p. 63) and that Jackson has exhibited a higher preference for black self-development than for integration (BLC pp. 57–58). Moreover, Paris reports that "Jackson emphasizes what Blacks should do for themselves ... and de-emphasizes what America should do for Blacks" (BLC p. 62). In this regard, Jackson's philosophy is consistent with the philosophy of black power. Paris goes on to observe that Jackson's concept of black self-development and independence is distinguished from that of many "Black nationalists" by its "vigorous patriotism" (BLC p. 63). Thus, the substance of Jackson's own philosophy of black self-development is consistent with the real denotative meaning of black power. But Jackson's rejection of black power is based upon his rejection of its connotative meaning (black racism), and upon a level of patriotism that distinguished him from almost all others in the black churches and communities.

Paris describes King's theological social ethical view as a "God-centered ethic" (BLC p. 85) based upon the parenthood of God and the kinship of all humans (BLC p. 79). Paris teaches us that it is King's view that oppressive racial discrimination and segregation are contrary to God's will, and we must "cooperate with God" (BLC p. 84) in eradicating this and other evil, including poverty and militarism (BLC p. 108). Paris maintains that, according to King, the methods of social action we employ must be in accord with God's loving purpose. In order for social action to be commensurate with this principle of love, it must be nonviolent (BLC p. 79). Furthermore, while King had high regard for the national ideals as set forth in the U.S. Constitution, King, unlike Jackson, recognized a higher moral law that can and did require disobedience to unjust laws (BLC pp. 87–89).

In regard to the philosophy of black power, Paris recognizes that King rejected the connotative meanings and aspects of black power philosophy and that King affirmed "the positive tenets of Black Power" (BLC p. 96).

Adam Clayton Powell, Jr.'s, theological and social ethical view is found by Paris to include the parenthood of God and the kinship of all humanity, and a commitment to struggle for freedom—freedom understood to include political empowerment through participation in democratic processes. But, as Paris points out, Powell's theology is not easily connected to his normative social ethical reflections in the area of politics (BLC p. 195). Powell is found to believe that the religious goal of the church is to "usher in the Kingdom of God here and now in this world." This religious goal has its political side (BLC p. 114). The political aspects of our existence require prudential judgments and compromises inadequate to religious standards of righteousness (BLC p. 194). Paris summarizes Powell's political understanding in terms of faithfulness to "two major political principles: constitutional democracy and participatory power of the masses" (BLC p. 124).

In regard to the language and philosophy of black power, Paris teaches us that Powell spoke in the language of black power (BLC p. 127). He publicly identified with the black power movement (BLC p. 135). He viewed the historical role of the black church as a precursor to contemporary black theology (BLC p. 124). Powell rejected violence, and considered civil disobedience to unjust laws morally righteous (BLC p. 127). Paris says:

> He viewed his entire political philosophy as commensurate with the Black Power thrust save for its implications regarding violence. . . . Theologically, Powell looked on Black Power as being consistent with the will of God. [BLC p. 137]

Powell, then, was among the first African-American Christian leaders to employ the language and philosophy of black power.

Paris's description of the theological social ethical thinking of Jackson, King, and Powell indicates that all three represent a commitment to the view that God is the parent of all humanity. Accordingly, all humans are morally obliged to act in ways that are consistent with this kindredness. Furthermore, Paris's description indicates that for these three ways of thinking, the way in which we judge our social actions to be consistent or inconsistent with this kindredness, and with God's will, is by reference to the standard of God's kingdom as given to us in the Christian witness to Jesus. In *The Social Teachings of the Black Churches*, Paris does a theological social analysis of the official documents of the leaders of two African-American denominations—the African Methodist Episcopal Church and the National Baptist Convention, U.S.A., with the understanding that they are representative of the other major denominations. Paris finds that, indeed, "the fundamental principle of the black Christian tradition is depicted most adequately in the biblical doctrine of the parenthood of God and the kinship of all peoples" (ST p. 10).

Paris's description of the social ethical thinking of Malcolm X indicates that Malcolm X also believed in the universal parenthood of God and the kinship of all humans. Paris quotes Malcolm X from *Malcolm X Speaks*:

> True Islam removes racism, because people of all colors and races who accept its religious principles and bow down to the one God, Allah, also automatically accept each other as brothers and sisters, regardless of differences in complexion. [BLC p. 150]

Malcolm X believed in the Islamic theological social ethical ideal of government and righteous leadership guided by submission to the will of God.

Paris describes Malcolm X as "one of the patron saints of the Black Power movement" (BLC p. 166). He points, for example, to Malcolm's influence as a factor in the SNCC orientation toward the black power slogan during the 1966 march with King (BLC p. 166). Paris goes on to point out:

> All the principles set forth in Malcolm's philosophy of Black nationalism were adopted by the Black Power movement. Such major principles as Black control of institutions and organizations in the Black community, exclusion of whites from Black organizations, Black separatism as a major objective, Black self-development, Black self-respect, the recovery of Black history became, in the Black Power movement, indisputable moral goals for determining action even as they were for Malcolm and his movement. [BLC p. 166]

Paris also points to the repudiation of the term "Negro" in favor of black, and African-American as an enduring contribution of Malcolm's influence upon the black power movement (BLC p. 166).

Another of Malcolm's contributions to our social ethical thinking is a more international and global perspective upon our liberation struggle. For Malcolm an exclusive focus upon first-class U.S. citizenship and civil rights is inadequate. The African-American experience and circumstance has a global context that has to do with a heritage of colonialism and neocolonial exploitation. Paris emphasizes Malcolm's broader perspective on poverty when he says of Malcolm:

> He viewed poverty among Blacks as an inevitable outcome of racism and poverty among darker peoples of the world as the result of racism's twin, colonialism. In his understanding, capitalism necessitates poverty, because it always needs blood to suck. [BLC p. 172]

On account of this more global perspective, Malcolm preferred to think in terms of a quest for "human rights" rather than in terms of "civil rights." Moreover, Malcolm advocated petitioning international authorities—United Nations, World Court—rather than exclusively U.S. civil authorities. Malcolm taught us that freedom and empowerment are not simply civil rights pertaining to U.S. citizens; they are human rights pertaining to the whole of oppressed humanity. Moreover, Malcolm asserted that Africans and African-Americans have a human right to develop independently empowered and internationally related political associations. In this regard, Malcolm's philosophy of black nationalism is consistent with the black church's separatist/pluralist tradition. The philosophy of black nationalism prescribes for the area of national and international politics what our churches have already achieved in the world of ecclesial relations—independently empowered and racially separate institutions and structures.

There are numerous other similarities and dissimilarities between the views of these four religious leaders. More of them than mentioned here are clearly outlined and carefully reflected upon by Paris in *Black Leaders in Conflict*. The theological and social views mentioned offer sufficient conceptual data for us to appreciate the reasonableness of Paris's conclusion—that all four social ethical views are to be affirmed, since they are mutually compatible and complementary visions of the African-American circumstance.

As Paris understands it, each of the four views contributes something to an adequate description of our circumstance. Each of the four views imply or explicate forms of social action that are important to the struggle for liberation. Based upon this "wholistic" vision, which affirms unity without denying diversity, Paris prescribes that the African-American leaders and communities represented by these four styles of thinking should recognize this unity and common ground. They should engage in loosely federated coalition efforts to improve upon the African-American circumstance through the exercise of diverse and complementary forms of black power. Paris maintains that these diverse styles of leadership "do not easily lend themselves to cooperative action," but he proposes that the place to find "the basis for concrete coalition" and "cooperative action" is "in some concrete moral issue, the eradication of which was desired by all four leaders" (BLC p. 196).

From Paris we learn that the one moral issue upon which all four leaders agree is that we must "struggle against poverty" (BLC p. 42). So again, this time by way of an analysis of four types of African-American religious social ethical thinking, we arrive at the conclusion that it is appropriate for our religious leaders to exercise various kinds of black power in national and international affairs in the struggle against economic powerlessness.

Charles V. Hamilton, in his book *The Black Preacher in America*, also identifies King, Jackson, Powell, and Malcolm X as representative of African-American religious leadership. However, Hamilton reminds us that this kind of national stature is exceptional among black preachers in the U.S. Hamilton says:

> One important fact about the black preacher is that he is essentially a local man. With the exception in modern times of only a handful like Martin King, Joseph H. Jackson, Adam Powell and Malcolm X, the primary effectiveness of the black preacher is at the community, church level. [BPA p. 224]

Given the fact that most black ministers and church leaders are primarily local leaders, the social ethical question of how best to break the bread that we control is a question that is more about the use and exercise of local resources than about national and international policies. Accordingly, Paris's point about the diverse yet complementary character of the social ethical views represented by four national leadership styles is improved when it is coupled with Hamilton's increased attention to the local and congregational levels. Additionally, the need for local leadership committed to a politics of black ethnicity and economic empowerment is suggested by Harold Cruse when he points to "a profound black leadership vacuum" between the national level where traditionally noneconomic liberal leadership types dominate and local community levels (PBE p. 361). We need bread breaking and economically empowering religious leadership on the local and congregational levels as well as on the national and international levels.

These reflections upon African-American leadership in social thought and action suggest the need for leadership committed to the struggle for empowerment through the sharing of power, bread, and other resources and opportunities. Clearly, the call for leadership that is committed to a social ethic of breaking bread, and which is committed to worshipful awareness of our struggle's relation to God, is a call appropriate to our religious and churchly vocations. Black theological social ethical reflection affirms that our churches, denominations, and various religious communities are uniquely qualified and morally obliged to offer diverse-unified-bread breaking-God-conscious leadership in social thought and action. Moreover, black theological social ethical reflection finds that it is appropriate for the black church to provide, as it sometimes does, the kinds of leadership that Cruse, Paris, and Hamilton prescribe. Their work indicates that there is an urgent need for African-American leadership that does not restrict its social ethical concerns to civil rights conceived as noneconomic liberalism and integration. Comprehensive social-cultural-political-economic empowerment, along with spiritual empowerment, is essential to our freedom, and to our ability to contribute to freedom for others.

THE BOTTOM LINE

Among the questions that a religious appropriation of the philosophy of black power calls us to consider is: What must we religious African-Americans do with our individual, congregational, and denominational resources in order to contribute to the comprehensive social, political, cultural, and economic empowerment of all the people? We know now that the bread we ought to break internationally, nationally, and locally includes leadership, money, food, jobs, land, housing, righteous education, and socialization (including the use of such resources as religious ritual, music, and dance), vastly increased attention to male-female-family-church relations, health care, child care, home care, family care, elder care, power, and other opportunities and resources essential to the nurture, survival, fruitful increase, and empowerment of all the people.

And moreover, the ecological sensitivity that we can harvest from the cultural gardens of traditional African and native American peoples, and from the gardens of other traditional peoples, calls us to see that the well-being of people is fully related to the well-being of other life. In order to contribute to the well-being of all the people, including those who are not yet born, we must contribute to the nurture and fruition of the whole living planet.

We know also that Christian religion calls us to increase prayerful awareness of God and right relationship to God, particularly awareness of God through awareness of and right relationship to the resurrected Jesus. The Gospel of Luke teaches us wherein we can perceive the presence of Jesus. In the 24th chapter of Luke we read that some days after the crucifixion, two of the apostles were walking to a village called Emmaus, which was seven miles away. We are told that the resurrected Jesus joined them in this walk, that he walked and talked with them all the way to Emmaus, but that the apostles did not recognize him. When they reached Emmaus, Jesus "made as though he would have gone further," but the apostles invited him to stay the evening with them in Emmaus. That evening Jesus, whom they still did not recognize, joined them at a meal. And when the bread had been broken and blessed, the eyes of the apostles were opened and they recognized him (Luke 24:30-31). Here, Jesus is recognized in the breaking of bread.

It is through the ethic of breaking bread that we empower the people to recognize our resurrected Lord. The bottom line of a black theological social ethical appropriation of the philosophy of black power is "Let us break bread together." Where bread is not broken, Jesus is not recognized, God is not served, and the people are not free.

NOTES

1. In a widely distributed cassette tape from around 1987, Na'im Akbar delivers a speech to a congregation of African-American university students. It is entitled "The Black Family as Black Power."

2. In chapter 3 – "The Sit-Ins Begin" – of *Civilities and Civil Rights: Greensboro, North Carolina, and the Black Struggle for Freedom*, William H. Chafe writes: "On February 1, 1960, four young men from North Carolina Agricultural and Technical College set forth on an historic journey that would ignite a decade of civil rights protest. Walking into downtown Greensboro, they entered the local Woolworth's, purchased toothpaste and other small items, and then sat at the lunch counter and demanded equal service with white persons ... Their actions sparked the student phase of the civil rights revolution. Within two months, the sit-in movement had spread to fifty-four cities in nine states. By mid-April, the Student Nonviolent Coordinating Committee (SNCC) had formed in Raleigh, North Carolina, to carry forward the battle. Within a year, more than one hundred cities had engaged in at least some desegregation of public facilities in response to student-led demonstrations. The 1960s stage of the freedom movement had begun." (CCR p. 71). Chafe reports that "two of the four initial demonstrators attended Shiloh Baptist Church, presided over by Otis Hairston, who had led the NAACP membership drive in 1959 and who provided mimeograph materials to the students when the demonstrations began" (CCR p. 81). Chafe identifies the four students as David Richmond, Franklin McCain, Ezell Blair, Jr. (Jibreel Khazan), and Joseph McNeil (CCR p. 84). Also see Taylor Branch's account of the significance of the Greensboro sit-ins for Martin Luther King, Jr., and the civil rights movement in chapter 7 – "The Quickening" – of *Parting the Waters: America in the King Years 1954-63*.

3. See Jon Michael Spencer, "Rhythm in Black Religion of the American Diaspora." Spencer argues that the diaspora "de-drummed the African, but it did not de-rhythmize him" (p. 67). "Although not completely deferred, the drum was definitely detached from its religious moorings" (p. 70). Also Spencer points out that rhythm – "the essential African remnant" – survives in African-American worship via hand clapping, and that religious dance survived the diaspora in the form of the ring-shout.

4. See Judith Lynne Hanna, *To Dance is Human: A Theory of Nonverbal Communications*.

5. Eugene, along with many black female theologians, chooses to indicate the difference between the perspective of black female theologians and that of white female theologians by using a term coined by Alice Walker to describe a liberated black woman – "womanist." The term "womanist" comes from Alice Walker's book, *In Search of Our Mothers' Gardens: Womanist Prose*. Also see Alice Walker's article

"In Search of Our Mothers' Gardens" (originally published in *MS.* magazine), in James H. Cone and Gayraud S. Wilmore's *Black Theology: A Documentary History, 1966-1979.* Taking a clue from Katie Geneva Cannon's use of Alice Walker's "womanist" language, we might describe black theology's appropriation of the social ethical agenda we have received from the black church women's movement as an inheritance from our mothers' garden. Cannon describes her own religious and womanist heritage in *Inheriting Our Mothers' Gardens: Feminist Theology in Third World Perspective*, edited by Letty M. Russell, Kwok Pui-lan, Ada Maria Isasi-Diaz, Katie Geneva Cannon. Also see Katie G. Cannon, "Moral Wisdom in the Black Women's Literary Tradition"; idem, *Black Womanist Ethics*; Jacquelyn Grant, *White Women's Christ and Black Women's Jesus: Feminist Christology and Womanist Response*; Jacqueline D. Carr-Hamilton, "Notes on the Black Womanist Dilemma"; Renita J. Weems, *Just a Sister Away: A Womanist Vision of Women's Relationships in the Bible*; and Delores S. Williams, "The Color of Feminism: Or Speaking the Black Woman's Tongue." For a black African alternative to the white feminist agenda, see Mercy Amba Oduyoye, "The Roots of African Christian Feminism." For feminist theological reflection upon the history of racist/white supremacist aspects of the nineteenth century Anglo-American suffrage movement, and analogously, of the current Anglo-American feminist movement, see Barbara H. Andolsen, *Daughters of Jefferson, Daughters of Bootblacks: Racism and American Feminism.* For critical reflection upon Andolsen's work by Renita J. Weems, Linda Mercadante, Marcia Riggs, and Victoria Byerly, along with Andolsen's response, see round table discussion on "Racism in the Women's Movement." Also see Miranda Davies, ed., *Third World Second Sex: Women's Struggles and National Liberation*; Angela Y. Davis, *Women, Culture and Politics*; Paula Giddings, *In Search of Sisterhood: Delta Sigma Theta and the Challenge of the Black Sorority Movement*; *When and Where I Enter: The Impact of Black Women on Race and Sex in America*; Gerda Lerner, ed., *Black Women in White America: A Documentary History*; and for a black lesbian feminist perspective, consult Audre Lorde's *Sister Outsider: Essays and Speeches.*

6. See A.C. Nielson's summary of "Television Viewing among Blacks" for January-February 1989 in *Nielsen Television Index News*. Here we are told that, "TV usage levels continue to be much higher in Black households than in all other. During the average week of January-February '89 the average Black household viewed 11.0 hours of TV per day while the average All Other viewed 7.2 hours."

7. Note that "Pope John Paul II has accused the mass media of being instruments of sin and spreading 'models of aberrant behavior' " (Associated Press report via *The Dallas Morning News*, Saturday, September 22, 1990).

8. See Lawrence N. Jones, "Transmitting the Faith: From Generation to Generation"; Katie Geneva Cannon, "Surviving the Blight"; Alice Walker's essay "In Search of Our Mothers' Gardens"; and Alice Walker's book, *In Search of Our Mothers' Gardens: Womanist Prose.*

9. Among many historical sources that display a long tradition of aggressive support for education on the part of African-American churches and denominations, see Leroy Fitts, *A History of Black Baptists*; Bishop William J. Walls, *African Methodist Episcopal Zion Church: Reality of the Black Church*; and David Henry Bradley, Sr., *A History of the A.M.E. Zion Church, Part II, 1872-1968.* Bradley's text gives a detailed account of the black colleges and schools founded and supported by the Zionist exercise of black power in the areas of education and socialization.

Also see Bradley's *A History of the A.M.E. Zion Church, Part I, 1796-1872.*

10. Many of us are coming to accept the fact that recent generations of African-American students have not been well served by past and present versions of "integration" in the public school systems. Harold Cruse points to E. Franklin Frazier's work from 1957 in demographic and social theory as indicating that there were "societal limits" to what it would be possible to implement in regard to integration of the public schools (PBE p. 202). Cruse finds that Frazier's work implied that because integration of elementary and high schools exceeded those limits—unlike professional and graduate schools—the effort to achieve integration of the public schools would fail (PBE p. 62). Finally Cruse quotes sociologist James S. Coleman as saying in 1983, "the assumption that integration would improve achievement of lower class black children has now been shown to be fiction" (PBE p. 396). Also see E. Franklin Frazier, *Black Bourgeoise* (New York: Free Press-Macmillan, 1957); and idem, *The Negro in the United States*, revised edition (New York: Macmillan, 1957).

11. David Maldonado's "African American and Hispanic Older Persons: A Preliminary Report on their Religiosity, Religious Participation and Attitudes toward the Church and Clergy" is an unpublished sociological study (July 1990). Maldonado concludes that "the church ought to be much more concerned about and in the practice of providing a holistic ministry," which addresses the needs of elderly African-Americans and Hispanics (p. 18).

12. Sheron C. Patterson's *Ministry with Black Single Adults* is a very fine pastoral response to the need for a church-based singles ministry that addresses the needs of African-American adults.

13. In *A History of the A.M.E. Zion Church, Part II, 1872-1968*, David Henry Bradley, Sr., writes: "As one looks back on the formation of Zion Methodism in the 18th Century it is not hard to discern at least six basic reasons for its birth: the necessity of a wider Christian fellowship among African believers and the descendants of Africans; the urgency of evangelism among this same group; the necessity of economic development among free black men and freed men; the advancement of social and educational concerns, including the working for the abolition of slavery; the development of an indigenous ministry; and the concern for expansion and development of Christian experience among black people" (p. 96). Note that the basic reasons for the birth of Zion Methodism include "the necessity of economic development" and "the advancement of social and educational concerns." According to Bradley's data, the early Zionist agenda for the exercise of black power is not the noneconomic liberalism that Cruse objects to. The early Zionist agenda is racially separatist, or pluralist, and it includes economic empowerment. So today's philosophy of black power can be received among Zionites as a call to recover and revitalize its early agenda. Bradley himself warns the denomination against "losing sight of the reasons for its existence" (p. 96).

BIBLIOGRAPHY

Aborampah, Osei-Mensah. "Black Male-Female Relationships: Some Observations." *The Journal of Black Studies* (March 1989).

Akbar, Na'im. "The Black Family as Black Power." This is the title of a widely distributed cassette tape recording of a speech by Akbar to a congregation of

African-American university students from around 1987.

Andolsen, Barbara H. *Daughters of Jefferson, Daughters of Bootblacks: Racism and American Feminism.* Macon, Ga.: Mercer University Press, 1986.

Bradley, David Henry. *A History of the A. M. E. Zion Church, Part I, 1796–1872.* Nashville: Parthenon Press, 1956, 1972.

———. *A History of the A. M. E. Zion Church, Part II, 1872–1968.* Nashville: Parthenon Press, 1970.

Branch, Taylor. *Parting the Waters: America in the King Years 1954–63.* New York: Simon and Schuster, 1988.

Brooks, Evelyn. "Religion, Politics, and Gender: The Leadership of Nannie Helen Burroughs." *The Journal of Religious Thought,* vol. 44, no. 2 (Winter-Spring 1988).

Cannon, Katie Geneva. *Black Womanist Ethics.* Atlanta: Scholars Press, 1988.

———. "Moral Wisdom in the Black Women's Literary Tradition." *The Annual of the Society of Christian Ethics* (1984).

———. "Surviving the Blight." *Inheriting Our Mothers' Gardens: Feminist Theology in Third World Perspective,* Letty M. Russell, Kwok Pui-lan, Ada Maria Isasi-Diaz, Katie Geneva Cannon, eds. Philadelphia: Westminster Press, 1988.

Carmichael, Stokely, and Charles V. Hamilton. *Black Power: The Politics of Liberation in America.* New York: Vintage Books, 1967.

Carr-Hamilton, Jacqueline D. "Notes on the Black Womanist Dilemma." *The Journal of Religious Thought,* vol. 45, no. 1 (Summer-Fall 1988).

Chafe, William H. *Civilities and Civil Rights: Greensboro, North Carolina, and the Black Struggle for Freedom.* New York: Oxford University Press, 1980.

Cruse, Harold. *Plural But Equal: A Critical Study of Blacks and Minorities in America's Plural Society.* New York: William Morrow, 1987.

Davies, Miranda, ed. *Third World Second Sex: Women's Struggles and National Liberation.* London: Zed Books, 1983.

Davis, Angela Y. *Women, Culture and Politics.* New York: Random House, 1984.

Eugene, Toinette M. "Moral Values and Black Womanists." *The Journal of Religious Thought,* vol. 44, no. 2. (Winter-Spring, 1988).

Fitts, Leroy. *A History of Black Baptists.* Nashville: Broadman Press, 1985.

Frazier, E. Franklin. *Black Bourgeoise.* New York: Free Press-Macmillan, 1957.

———. *The Negro in the United States,* revised edition. New York: Macmillan, 1957.

Giddings, Paula. *In Search of Sisterhood: Delta Sigma Theta and the Challenge of the Black Sorority Movement.* New York: William Morrow, 1988.

———. *When and Where I Enter: The Impact of Black Women on Race and Sex in America.* New York: Bantam Books, 1984, 1985.

Grant, Jacquelyn. *White Women's Christ and Black Women's Jesus: Feminist Christology and Womanist Response.* Atlanta: Scholars Press, 1989.

Hamilton, Charles V. *The Black Preacher in America.* New York: William Morrow, 1972.

Hanna, Judith Lynne. *To Dance is Human: A Theory of Nonverbal Communications.* Chicago: University of Chicago Press, 1987.

Hare, Nathan and Julia, eds. *Crisis in Black Sexual Politics.* San Francisco: Black Think Tank, 1989.

Jones, Harry H. "The Crisis in Negro Leadership." *Crisis,* vol. 19, no. 5 (March 1920).

Jones, Lawrence N. "Transmitting the Faith: From Generation to Generation." *The Journal of Religious Thought,* vol. 46, no. 1 (Summer-Fall 1989).

Lerner, Gerda, ed. *Black Women in White America: A Documentrary History.* New York: Vintage Books, 1973.

Lorde, Audre. *Sister Outsider: Essays and Speeches.* Trumansburg, N.Y.: Crossing Press, 1984.

Maldonado, David. "African American and Hispanic Older Persons: A Preliminary Report on their Religiosity, Religious Participation and Attitudes toward the Church and Clergy." Unpublished (July 1990).

Nielson, A. C. "Summary of 'Television viewing among Blacks' " for January-February 1989. *Nielsen Television Index News.* New York: Nielson Media Research, 1989.

Oduyoye, Mercy Amba. "The Roots of African Christian Feminism." *Variations in Christian Theology in Africa,* John S. Pobee and Carl F. Hallencreutz, eds. Nairobi, Kenya: Uzima Press, 1986.

Paris, Peter J. *Black Leaders in Conflict: Joseph H. Jackson, Martin Luther King, Jr., Adam Clayton Powell, Jr., Malcolm X.* New York: Pilgrim Press, 1978.

———. *The Social Teachings of the Black Churches.* Philadelphia: Fortress Press, 1985.

Patterson, Sheron C. *Ministry with Black Single Adults.* Nashville: Discipleship Resources, 1990.

Roberts, J. Deotis. *Roots of a Black Future: Family and Church.* Philadelphia: Westminster Press, 1980.

Smith, Wallace Charles. *The Church in the Life of the Black Family.* Valley Forge, Pa.: Judson Press, 1985, 1988.

Spencer, Jon Michael. "Rhythm in Black Religion of the American Diaspora." *The Journal of Religious Thought,* vol. 44, no. 2 (1988).

Walker, Alice. "In Search of Our Mothers' Gardens." *Black Theology: A Documentary History, 1966-1979,* Gayraud S. Wilmore and James H. Cone, eds. Maryknoll, N.Y.: Orbis Books, 1979, 1984 (originally published in *MS.,* vol. 2, no. 11, May 1974).

———. *In Search of Our Mothers' Gardens: Womanist Prose.* San Diego: Harcourt Brace Jovanovich, 1983.

Walls, Bishop William J. *African Methodist Episcopal Zion Church: Reality of the Black Church.* Charlotte, N.C.: A. M. E. Zion Publishing House, 1974.

Weems, Renita J. *Just a Sister Away: A Womanist Vision of Women's Relationships in the Bible.* San Diego: LuraMedia, 1988.

———. "Racism in the Women's Movement." *The Journal of Feminist Studies in Religion,* vol. 4, no. 1 (Spring 1988).

Williams, Delores S. "The Color of Feminism: Or Speaking the Black Woman's Tongue." *The Journal of Religious Thought,* vol. 43, no. 1 (Spring-Summer 1986).

X, Malcolm. *Malcolm X Speaks,* George Breitman, ed. New York: Grove Press, 1965.

Postscript

In 1987, when I first began work on *Empower the People*, I had already determined that this social ethical reflection would be framed in large part by that black churchly appropriation of the philosophy of black power that has come to be called black theology. Furthermore, the early formulations of the philosophy of black power from the 1960s, and subsequent black churchly appropriations of black power, gave me reason to expect that a black theological social ethical reflection would include considerable attention to political and economic matters. What I was not expecting was so much attention directed to matters of problematic black male-female relations. To be sure, most of those scholars in the theological community who had occasion to review this manuscript prior to its publication were equally surprised at this aspect of its content. There were even those (not every one of them white, and none of them mentioned by name in this text) who advised me that such matters were trivial and not worthy of serious scholarly attention. The witness of the scholarly literature produced by African-American social scientists during the 1980s, and the witness of the people and their music, and the witness of my own black experiences testify to the contrary.

My own experience is such that I can claim no exception to many of the problems described under the category of problematic black male-female relations. During the ten months that passed between the time when this text was basically complete and the moment at which this postscript was composed, I have had time enough away from the scholarly findings to engage in more personal reflection upon the significance of what the social scientific literature has taught me about my own social location. At this point I speak not so much as a theologian, social analyst, or scholar, but simply as an ordinary black man who has discovered that his so-called personal problems are among the most common features of contemporary African-American existence. My latest reflection upon this circumstance is a combination of good and bad news.

The good news, which I report from personal observation and experience rather than from scholarly research, is that for all the difficulties and problems that exist between black men and women, we still somehow manage to be very much in love with each other. The bad news is that we do not trust each other. It is an altogether ordinary experience for black men to discover that while our women love us deeply, they seldom trust us. Our women have not much confidence in our willingness or ability to fulfill their expectations. Where with regard to white America, there is neither love nor trust for black men; with regard to black women, for us there is much love, but little trust. This seemingly ever present vote of no confidence shadows our day-to-day existence.

This problematic feature of black male existence is distinct from but not separable from the social, political, and economic difficulties described throughout the socio-scientific literature of the 1980s. Nathan and Julia Hare, and many other African-American social analysts, are correct in emphasizing the connections between problematic black male-female-family relations and the problems of black political and economic empowerment. Given these connections, it is likely that research will reveal that black and colored and similarly oppressed peoples in other places are experiencing similar difficulties. It is my hope that our brothers and sisters in other places, and perhaps at other times, will be warned about the ways in which issues of comprehensive socio-economic and political empowerment impact matters of male-female-family-tribal relations. In particular, I hope that our sisters and brothers in southern Africa and the front-line states will learn from the unfortunate legacy of what Harold Cruse calls "non-economic liberalism." The kinds of political and civil rights strategies that fail to include land and powers of economic decision-making have been inadequate to our struggles, and they are likely to be inadequate to other liberation struggles.

The sociological data concerning the present and future circumstances of African-Americans in the United States are bad news. According to these data, most of us are among the communities of the oppressed. It is bad news that there are truly disadvantaged populations, and it is bad news that so many of us are among the truly disadvantaged. From the perspective of black theology, the good news is that—in the words of James Cone—God is "God of the oppressed." While the bad news is such as may call for lamentation and tears of frustration and anger, the good news is such as can bring (paraphrasing a line from Stevie Wonder's music) "joy inside our tears." Speaking of God as God of the oppressed is speaking a word of condemnation and wrath for all acts of oppression, and to all who benefit from oppressive circumstances and structures. On the other hand, to speak of God as God of the oppressed is also to sound a note of joy, gospel, and liberation for those who are oppressed and for the church that joins the poor and oppressed in their struggles for freedom and empowerment. Black theological social ethics must be about the business of "speaking the truth," which is bad news in some respects and good news in other respects. In accordance with black churchly appropriations of the philosophy of black power, and in accordance with black power's emphasis upon what black folk can do to contribute to the comprehensive empowerment of all the people, our prescriptive emphasis has been upon the good news—that we are not powerless, that there is much that we can do, and that there is a

God who sides with us in our struggle for freedom and comprehensive empowerment.

Another matter that gains new significance from retrospective reflection concerns the role of the Reverend Doctor Martin Luther King, Jr. Most historical accounts of the development of the philosophy of black power fail to acknowledge the fact that King was one of its early contributors. Instead, one is usually given to believe that King opposed the philosophy of black power. Such a view is contrary to the historical facts. As we saw in chapter 2, such a view is contrary to King's own witness in *Where Do We Go From Here: Chaos or Community*. Quiet as it is commonly kept, one of the significant historical truths underlined in this work is the fact that King was one of the early architects of the modern philosophy of black power. Moreover, King's social ethical prescriptions for coalition efforts to abolish poverty are among the most radical of those we have considered.

Index

Aborampah, Osei-Mensah, 88-90, 104
Abraham, 6, 20
Adam, 6
African Civilizations, 3
African National Congress, 7
AIDS, 65
Akbar, Na'im, 103
Akhenaten, 3, 5
Aldridge, Delores P., 87, 90
Allen, Richard, 9, 28
Asante, M. K., 89
Bernards, Jessie, 88
Bethune, Mary M., 107-8
Beyond Preference, 37
Billingsley, A., 88
Black boys, 87
Black consciousness, 6
Black family, 79-81
Black inferiority, 5
Black leadership, 112-19
Black Leaders in Conflict, 113-14, 118
Black male-female conflict, 79-85, 87, 12
Black music, 77-78, 81, 104-6
Black nationalism, 26-28
Black power, 5, 12-13, 22, 24, 26, 29, 38, 42, 73, 89, 103, 115-16, 127, 129
Black Power: The Politics of Liberation, 11, 26, 29, 54, 93
"Black Power Statement," 12
The Black Preacher in America, 119
Black religion, 12, 28
Black Religion and Black Radicalism, 9, 28
Black teenage pregnancy, 59
Black theology, 13, 17n12, 22, 127
Black Theology and Black Power, 13
Black Theology of Liberation, 13, 115
Black women, 47

Branch, Taylor, 115
Bread, 34-35, 102
Bringing the Black Boy to Manhood, 86
The Broken Patriarchy, 87
Brooks, Evelyn, 107
Brown, Charlotte H., 107-8
Burroughs, Nannie H., 107-8
Cancer, Tropic of, 3-5, 7, 10
Cannon, Katie G., 109
Capricorn, Tropic of, 3-4
Carmichael, Stokely, 11-13, 25-26, 29, 37-38, 54-55, 103, 108
The Church in the Life of the Black Family, 111
Clark, Kenneth B., 40
Cleaver, Kathleen, 82
Coalition, 42, 52, 54
Cone, James H., 13, 75, 114, 128
Congress of Racial Equality, 25
Connah, Graham, 3-4
Conservatism, 36
Cornelius, Don, 76
Crisis in Black Sexual Politics, 87
Cruse, Harold, 92-94, 112-13, 119, 128
Dance, 104-6
D'Aquili, E. G., 89
The Declining Significance of Race, 39
Dewey, John, 37
To Die For the People, 57
Disobedience, civil, 115
Douglass, Frederick, 23
Drugs, 64-65
DuBois, W. E. B., 56, 59, 92, 99n10, 112
Edelman, Marian W., 47, 58, 90-91
Emancipation Proclamation, 23
Employment, 89
Empowerment, 24, 30, 34, 66, 103, 108
Empower the People, 111-12

The Endangered Black Family, 79, 82, 86
Ethic of breaking bread, 35-36, 48, 52, 55-56, 102, 120
Ethic of crumbs, 35, 55-56
Ethics, 10
Eugene, Toinette M., 107
Eve, 2, 6, 14n2
Family liberation, 110-12, 128
Farrakham, Louis, Minister, 76
Franklin, C. W., II, 88-89
Frazier, E. Franklin, 40
Freedom, 20
Gamwell, Franklin I., 37
Gandhi, Mohandas, 114
Garnet, Henry H., Rev., 28
Garvey, Marcus, 7, 8, 92
"Gladiator schools," 66-67, 84
God, 20, 102, 117
Gonzalez, Lawrence, 66
Government, 43
Hairston, Owen, Rev., 8, 35-36
Hamilton, Charles V., 11, 13, 26, 37-38, 43-44, 54-55, 119
Harding, Vincent, 11, 74
Hare, Julia and Nathan, 78-85, 90, 109, 128
Hill, Robert B., 44-47, 48, 58
Hulbert, Ann, 89
Imprisonment, 65-67
Income, guaranteed, 53
Inheriting Our Mothers' Gardens, 109
Jackson, J., 88
Jackson, Jesse, Rev., 76
Jackson, Joseph H., 113-16, 119
Jacob, John E., 42-43
Jerusalem, 75
Jesus, 6, 22, 120-21
Jones, Harold H., 112
Jones, Lawrence N., 109
Jones, Quincy, 78
Joshua, 21
Jubilee, 22
King, Martin Luther, Jr., 12, 23-26, 29, 52-53, 57, 109, 113, 119, 129
Kingdom of God, 22
Krishna, Lord, 5
Kunjufu, Jawanza, 87, 90
Lazarus, 35

Lee, Spike, 77-78
Liberalism, 36-37
Liberty, 37
Lincoln, C. Eric, 48
Locke, John, 36
Malcolm X, 4, 26, 109, 113, 117-19
Marriage rate among U.S. blacks, 60-64
Matthew, 22
McKissick, Floyd, 25, 26-28, 29, 53-54
Meredith, James, 25, 29
Mill, John Stuart, 36
Minority, 6
Modernization, political, 54
Moses, 6, 20
Moynihan, Daniel, 40, 59
National Baptist Convention, 115, 117
National Committee of Black Churchmen, 12
National Committee of Negro Churchmen, 12
National Urban League, 42, 55, 58-59, 83
Newton, Huey P., 57
Noah, 6
Nonviolence, 67
Paris, Peter J., 113-14, 116-19
"Parity 2000," 42-43, 56
Parting the Waters, 115
Pharaoh, 6, 20
Plural But Equal, 92, 112
Powell, Adam C., Jr., 113, 116, 119
Prophecy, 14
Protestant, 8-9
Religion, 103-6, 108
Revolution, black church, 9
Ricks, Willie, 12, 25
Rites of passage, 89-90, 103, 106
Roberts, J. Deotis, 110-11
Robinson, Marion B., Rev., 8
Roddenberry, Gene, 6
Roots of a Black Future, 111
Rustin, Bayard, 40-41
Smith, Adam, 36
Smith, Wallace C., 111-12
The Social Teachings of the Black Churches, 113, 117
Sociology, 38

Southern Christian Leadership Conference, 25
Speaking the Truth, 75
Staples, Robert, 88-89
The State of Black America 1989, 42, 56
Stewart, James B., 77
Swinton, David, 43
There is a River, 11, 74
Three Fifths of a Man, 26-27, 29
Ture, Kuame. See Stokely Carmichael
The Truly Disadvantaged, 40, 58
Turner, Nat, 28
Tutankhamen, 3, 5
Unemployment, 45
Universal Negro Improvement Association, 7, 16n7
Urban League. *See* National Urban League

U.S. citizens, 56
Walker, Alice, 109
Walker, David, 28
Walker, Mary Edna Woods, 1
Walker, Theodore D., Rev., 1
Walker's Appeal, 28
Washington, Booker T., 92
Washington, Denzel, 76
Where Do We Go From Here, 23-25, 26-27, 29, 129
White Supremacy, 3, 5, 7
Whitfield, Norman, 78
Wilmore, Gayraud 5, 9, 28
Wilson, William Julius, 38-42, 55, 59, 83
Wonder, Stevie, 78, 128
Woods, Hugh, 2, 14n1
Woods, Moses D., I, 1, 14n1
Woods, Zebulon Vance, 1

www.ingramcontent.com/pod-product-compliance
Lightning Source LLC
Chambersburg PA
CBHW072153160426
43197CB00012B/2365